Culture is the single mo~~st~~ rga-
nization. It impacts morale, ~~loyalty,~~ vice,
and productivity. Whether you want to transform a p~~oor cu~~ ~~m~~dify
a stellar one, I strongly suggest you read this book.

> **RANDY ROSS**, Founder and CEO of Remarkable!;
> author of *Remarkable!* and *Relationomics*

Chief Culture Officer is an employee engagement odyssey chock-full of business anecdotes, wisdom, and practical application. A fast-moving read from Dan Behm, who builds the case that a company's people are its greatest asset, sums up the point with the assertion, "Happy employees are productive employees." Hats off to OST's tremendous success! We need more companies like OST and successful people leaders like Behm. I highly recommend *Chief Culture Officer* to any small business or Fortune 500 leader in need of a culture building road map.

> **PRESTON POORE**, Director, The Coca-Cola Company;
> Co-owner, Numerica Corporation

Dan Behm's personal journey from a start-up to a successful business provides profound insights into the significance of culture—perhaps the hottest topic today, not only in business but also in society as a whole. Rather than thinking of culture as a utopian idea or a nebulous concept, Dan provides many practical examples of how each one of us can create a positive culture within our organizations and achieve remarkable outcomes.

> **SANJAY GUPTA**, Eli and Edythe L. Broad Dean of the Eli Broad
> College of Business, Michigan State University

In a world where the word *culture* is overused, Dan Behm and his team at OST have redefined what great culture looks and feels like. Every page of *Chief Culture Officer* made me feel like I was being mentored by my favorite and very successful uncle, a pure gift.

> **RON KITCHENS**, CEO, Southwest Michigan First; author of *Uniquely You:*
> *Transform Your Organization by Becoming the Leader Only You Can Be* (forthcoming)

Many years ago, as I was about to be given the reigns for my first CEO role in a large, multinational company, my chairman gave me some sage advice: "Remember, it's about the people and the culture you create that will make you win or lose." I wish now that I had had Mr. Behm's book then.

This book is simply amazing. An easy read that can be absorbed in one sitting. This book should be required reading for all MBA programs throughout the university system in the U.S. It is not only for business but for many other disciplines. What a great read!

> **FRANK J. FERACO**, Founding Partner, Isleworth Capital Partners LLC;
> former President of the Kohler Company and Emerson Electric Company

Technology is changing the world rapidly. Dan Behm and his company are changing business culture even faster, and Dan has given us an in-depth look at how that happened. I like to think that this book gives us insight into their "secret sauce." That secret sauce has standard ingredients of business success, but also important new ingredients that make business results even more rewarding. *Chief Culture Officer* is a "must read" for any aspiring entrepreneur or business leader.

PETER M. PEREZ, President and CEO, Grand Rapids Symphony; former President, Steinway & Sons

Give Respect to Get Respect. You don't build a business, you build people, and then people build a business. There is No "I" in Team. These statements are simple philosophies but often difficult to execute in the workplace. A company's culture has a tremendous effect on whether a business succeeds or fails. Whether you're a sports organization or a small business, culture trumps everything.

In *Chief Culture Officer*, Dan Behm shares the ultimate blueprint to building a strong foundation for your business. He offers a straightforward, easy-to-read guide for maneuvering the corporate minefield. While the path to success is never straight, this book details how entrepreneurs and business leaders can build an employee-first culture to maximize profits. With this book you'll understand the real connection between employee engagement and performance—the secret to a powerful team.

STEVE SMITH, Basketball Analyst for Turner Sports; former 14-year NBA Player and World Champion; Olympic Gold Medalist

Dan is the Patch Adams of CEO culture builders. Through great storytelling and humor, Dan illustrates what's needed to build a culture that is high-performance, people-centered, and fun! As a customer, I was aware of the great work and outstanding people that OST was known for, but this book reveals the deliberate practices deployed by Dan and his team to build a culture that has a sustainable competitive advantage.

Leaders are often willing to share their success stories and what you should do. Dan goes a step further and, in his humble way, shares what didn't work and things you should avoid. Dan outlines how fear and failure are natural parts of the leadership journey and should not deter you from chasing your dreams or leading with humanity.

Whether you are a start-up trying to decide what you want your organization to become or a seasoned leader, you will find inspiration, good ideas, and a few hearty laughs in this book.

BRIAN C. WALKER, President and CEO, Herman Miller, Inc.

CHIEF
CULTURE
OFFICER

DAN BEHM

CHIEF
CULTURE
OFFICER

ATTRACT TOP TALENT,
GROW LIKE CRAZY, AND
HAVE AN INSANE AMOUNT OF FUN
DOING IT

credo
house publishers

Chief Culture Officer
Copyright © 2018 by Dan Behm
All rights reserved.

Published in the United States by Credo House Publishers,
a division of Credo Communications, LLC, Grand Rapids, Michigan
credohousepublishers.com

ISBN (Hardcover): 978-1-625860-98-9
ISBN (Softcover): 978-1-625861-08-5
ISBN (MOBI): 978-1-625861-09-2
ISBN (EPUB): 978-1-625861-10-8

Cover design by LUCAS Art & Design
Interior design and typesetting by Sharon VanLoozenoord
Editing by Elizabeth Banks

Printed in the United States of America

First edition

To my Mother, who has never stopped believing in me,

and

To my Grandmother Swannie, who prayed on her knees for each individual in our family every day of our lives.

Contents

Introduction

Why Should You Care?

A stranger seated next to a teen on an airplane turned to her and said, "Let's talk. I've heard that flights go quicker if you strike up a conversation with your fellow passenger."

The girl, who had just opened her book, closed it slowly and said to the stranger, "What would you like to talk about?"

"Oh, I don't know," said the stranger, smiling. "How about nuclear power?"

"Okay," she said, "that could be an interesting topic. But let me ask you something first. A horse, a cow, and a deer all eat the same stuff—grass—yet a deer excretes little pellets, while a cow turns out a flat patty, and a horse produces clumps of dried grass. Why do you suppose that is?"

The stranger, surprised by the girl's question, thought about it and said, "Hmmm, I have no idea."

To which the teen replied, "Do you really feel qualified to discuss nuclear power when you don't know crap?"

Special Place—Special People

It kind of felt that way when we opened our doors for business in January 1997. I had no experience running a technology company, managing people, or even an inkling of what made a great business culture. What I did have was a tenacious desire to succeed. Eighteen years later we had a lot to be thankful for:

180 talented employees
An incredibly dedicated leadership team

A compounded growth rate of 30 percent over for eleven years
Revenues of $166 million
Countless awards

All this has exceeded my wildest imagination. In the early years, like every entrepreneurial start-up, we were in survival mode. As time progressed we developed our own unique personality and way of doing things. We didn't think we were creating anything special along the way. We just wanted to have fun doing our jobs and see everyone we came into contact with have an equally enjoyable experience. We also had a deep desire to do things the right way.

Ultimately, Open Systems Technologies (OST) did become a special place with special people and a culture worth talking about. A place where employees can grow and prosper. A place where they can be themselves without concern for company politics. A place where they feel welcome and secure. It sounds more like a family than a company, and that's no accident.

The Secret to Our Success

Our employees are our top priority. We have a unique method of doing business and interacting with one another. Our theory is if we take care of our employees and the people they care about, they'll take care of our clients, and everything else will take care of itself.

This culture is part of us, it defines us.

Our emphasis on culture has led to extremely high levels of employee satisfaction. Our employees are polled every six months, and the question we weight the most is this: "If someone asked me if OST was a great place to work, my answer would be ____." Employees can answer either yes or no. In our most recent poll, 92 percent of our employees said yes and the average over several years is 95 percent.

I'm frequently asked about the secret to OST's success. Our leaders unanimously agree that our culture of placing employees and their families first is at the heart of it. We want to be profitable, sure, but we also want to be sustainable. We want to enjoy all the effort we pour into our jobs—but we need to believe we're part of something bigger than just bringing home a paycheck.

We never assume we've cracked the code for the perfect culture. It's more art than science, and so we'll never be completely satisfied with our culture. It is an ongoing process that requires constant nurturing and attention. Never being satisfied is part of what makes for a truly dynamic culture. We're the pebble in our own shoe.

You may not have heard of OST before picking up this book, but I hope you'll find our company culture worthy of consideration— quirky, surprising, productive, and even inspiring.

I wrote this book because I believe we have managed to build something unique and uniquely healthy. I'll offer a few insights, a lot of stories, and a handful of suggestions for what we believe makes a dynamic relational business environment. It would be a compliment to OST's hard work and creativity if you come away with an idea or two that you could apply to your own company's culture.

Instead of me rambling on in my own words, I thought it would be best to close with a random selection of quotes from our staff:

"You and Mer and Jim have done an incredible job creating what I think is the best possible work environment. This is a company that I truly love and feel blessed to be a part of. Thank you for extending the opportunity and for being not only an effective and strong leader, but an available and empathetic leader. The leadership exhibited by OST encourages me within my own growth and that is something special. You should be proud of the legacy you have built." —RICHARD

"OST has touched so many people's lives in many ways. Not many companies would have said yes to a couple of developers saying they want to make video games. The fact that you never laughed Aaron and me out of the room and we now have OST Games started means so much." —LARRY

"Thank you for the opportunity that OST has provided for me to continue to grow as a consultant and project manager. This is by far the best company that I have ever worked for and you should be proud of your accomplishments. You have impacted a lot of people and their families!" —LEE

"I know I've said this before, but thank you, sincerely, for your generosity. OST wouldn't have great employees if it weren't for the great leadership you guys provide. I know I speak for probably everyone at OST when I say the bonuses are very much appreciated, but it's your continued display of happiness, care for the people at OST, and willingness to listen to everyone (not just a chosen few) that has earned my respect and admiration. It's truly an honor to work with, and for, you all. Thank you!" —MATT

A Brief Note on Chapter Theme Songs

I love music, and it's a big part of the OST culture. Whenever we host a big event or throw a party, we crank it up! Every year at our company kickoff an employee band welcomes everyone at 8:30 a.m. with rock and roll—what a great way to start the day! That's why I've chosen a theme song for each chapter. It's fun! Each song will give you a sense for that chapter's overall message, but mostly I've included them for entertainment value. Enjoy.

PART ONE

THE COMPANY WE KEEP

History, Leadership, and Ownership

Company Unleashed

Facing Down the Terrifying Decision
to Buy Open Systems Technologies

CHAPTER THEME SONG:
"SHOULD I STAY OR SHOULD I GO," THE CLASH

Entrepreneurship in America is filled with fascinating stories of businesses that started in garages—our story begins in a basement.

In the fall of 2002, with the economy still reeling from the effects of 9/11, our leadership team had a tough decision to make: should we risk our parent company shutting us down, or make the move to purchase what was then a floundering company? If they closed the company we would lose our jobs. If we purchased the company we could each forfeit everything we owned.

History is peppered with examples of momentous decisions that have changed the world—for better and for worse. In 1959 Buddy Holly, Ritchie Valens, and The Big Bopper chartered a small plane to expedite their journey. The decision to board that fatal plane was one that forever changed the face of music. It was later memorialized in the song American Pie as "the Day the Music Died."

On August 29, 1963, a man finished a speech he had prepared, but was so impassioned that he continued to speak—the remainder of the speech will ever be known as the "I Have a Dream" speech—the man was Martin Luther King Jr.

Have you made a decision that changed the trajectory of your life?

We had started OST, an information technology company in Grand Rapids, Michigan, as a division of G/S Leasing located in Troy, Michigan. My business partner Jim VanderMey and I had a 30 percent stake in the company and were contemplating an offer for G/S's 70 percent. Our company, which focused on hardware, software, and IT services, had been losing money since 9/11; these were scary times for the nation and for our company.

We put our heart, soul, and every ounce of energy into OST and now had very little to show for it. We could claim fifteen employees in 1999, but were now down to seven. Our sales during the first year of operation were $6 million, but we had not exceeded that figure in any of the five years since. Regardless of our struggles to survive, OST was our baby and we wouldn't give her up easily.

It eventually became clear that G/S was going to shut us down. What should we do? Allow them to close the doors? Attempt to start a company of our own? If so, could we still fly under the OST name? How would our clients react? Should we go our separate ways? Find new jobs? So many questions and so few answers. We were afraid.

A Momentous Meeting

I spent days preparing for the meeting trying to anticipate everything our team might be thinking. A quote came to mind from F. Scott Fitzgerald's, *The Beautiful and Damned*: "I don't want just words. If that's all you have for me, you'd better go." I needed to present a substantial case or the group would not buy it, but all I had was words—and one simple graph.

Then came the time: fish or cut bait. Jim, Meredith, Brent, Bhaskar, Al, Kipp, and I gathered in the basement of my house on Grenelefe Drive with the intention of deciding the fate of OST. Little did they know I'd made up my mind before the meeting started:

I planned for all of us to purchase OST from the parent company G/S Leasing. And I needed them to be "all in" with me.

My logic was relatively simple. I built a graph that showed one bar with our monthly expenses, which were mostly salaries. Below the expense bar was a second bar that showed our monthly income. My argument was that 80 percent of our monthly expenses were covered by billable services which were fairly consistent every month. That left only 20 percent to be covered by product sales, and anything beyond that would be profit.

It was an emotional meeting, but eventually everyone agreed this made sense, the level of risk seemed tolerable. After hours of debate we decided to approach the owners of G/S Leasing to see if they were willing to sell OST.

Over the years we had approached G/S twice about the purchase of OST and their answer had been no. The third time was a charm, and from their perspective it must have felt like getting money out of a sinking ship. The deal was based on a company value of $500,000, which meant we would be required to pay them $350,000 cash (we already owned 30 percent). Each person's ownership would be based on the percentage of funding they contributed.

Now we just needed to come up with the money.

All In

Based on OST's results to that point, no businessperson in her right mind would have predicted our success. Not a bank in the world would give us a loan, so we had to get creative.

Buying in for some would mean giving up their life savings. For another it was a loan from parents, and for another it meant borrowing from a 401K retirement plan. Somehow we miraculously came up with the entire $350,000. It felt like a high-stakes game of "Texas Hold 'em" as we pushed every chip we could find to the center of the table. One by one each of us went "all in." As new owners with everything at stake, we had fire in our eyes and used our setbacks as motivation to win. But determination did not eliminate doubt. We were scared before. Now that we had invested our life savings, we were, in a word, terrified.

Breathe, we told ourselves. Put one foot in front of the other.

First we set financial goals for the next year and got everyone on the same page. If we could make a modest profit to help with cash flow, we would be thrilled. We put on game faces with our clients, knowing we had to exude confidence so that they would continue to do business with us.

We were pleasantly surprised that every one of our clients did so. Good for them . . . and great for us. This took some of the pressure off. Also, making our own decisions without needing to get approval from an out-of-town parent company invigorated our energies. As a subsidiary, we had felt handcuffed at times and now we were free. In all fairness to G/S—they were in a tough spot. OST was losing money, so G/S felt they needed to steer our decisions. That was hard because our businesses were different—they were not involved with the day-to-day operations of our business and were geographically distant.

It wasn't long before the business was gaining momentum beyond anything we had experienced previously. We were making better choices, taking far less time, and enjoying a competitive advantage. That first year on our own, our goal was $5 million in revenue and $300,000 in net profit. Our actual results were $5.5 million in revenue and $600,000 in net profit. Once we had our legs under us, we were off and running—growing at 30 percent, compounded annually, for eleven years.

Looking Back . . .

Gathered in my basement in 2002, making the decision to risk everything for our crazy little company, we never dreamed we would be part of something as unique as OST has turned out to be. Our company is not perfect, of course, but we're genuinely grateful for what OST has become.

I'm writing this thirteen years after that basement meeting, five of our seven founders are still with the company and I have recently retired, but remain on the Board of Directors. A lot has changed, and yet a lot has remained the same. The original five are still humble, family-focused people. We are all thankful for each other and the unconditional friendships, deep trust, and immense respect we have for one another. We're proud of what we've accomplished. These days we probably should be taking more time to just enjoy what we've built together. And sometimes we do!

So What Does This Mean to You?

If you have subsidiary businesses in different geographical locations, try to let them make their own decisions as much as possible. If you try to control them too much, it can deflate them and take the joy out of their jobs. Provide them with high-level direction and specific expectations, but let them run the day-to-day operations of the business without interference. They will be much more likely to take pride and complete ownership of the businesses they are running—and as a result provide better financial results.

If you are about to make a big decision like purchasing a company, it is okay to be afraid. A healthy amount of fear guards against inactivity and often leads to success. Sometimes a decision not to move ahead is the right one, but remember that no one ever made it big by saying no. There are some nonnegotiables; the business needs to be viable and the people need to be compatible. Consider and accept the worst-case scenario; failure. I don't know of anyone who has been wildly successful in business that has not also failed multiple times. Go big, or go home.

2

It All Comes Down to Trust

Building a Solid Leadership Team

CHAPTER THEME SONG:
"A MATTER OF TRUST," BILLY JOEL

Alexander the Great, one of the most powerful men in history, once led his troops across a hot, arid desert. After nearly two weeks of marching, he and his soldiers were near death from thirst, yet Alexander pushed ahead. During the scorching afternoon heat, two of his scouts brought what little water they were able to find. It barely filled a cup. Alexander's troops were shocked when he poured the water into the sand.

Legend has it that the great king and military commander said, "It is of no use for one to drink when many thirst." By not setting himself above his men, Alexander established a special bond with them.

Manipulating your leadership team to get what you want does not work. Your actions must be genuine, heartfelt, and in the best interest of everyone. The same is true with how your leadership team treats their people.

Actions, like Alexander pouring the water, are much more powerful than words and build the ultimate in trust.

Building a Leadership Team

Our success at OST all sounds pretty great now. We talk about how Meredith Bronk (COO), Jim VanderMey (CTO), and I (president) had the ultimate in complementary skill sets, as if it were planned that way. As if our business model anticipated the market increases and profit margins precisely. As if we knew all along that we would provide each other with the perfect synergistic balance.

But here's the truth behind the complementary skill sets: we lucked out. The good news is: you don't have to. You can learn from what happened to us by accident and build a leadership team to be well balanced from the start.

In the simplest terms, Jim was the technology person, Meredith was the operations person, and I was the businessperson. We think differently and each of us brought something unique to the table. If any one of us had started up OST and run it alone, I believe it would have failed miserably. With Meredith at the helm, we would have a great culture, quality processes, exceptional follow-through—and no sales. If Jim were solo, we would have supertalented teams of people developing game-changing technology solutions—and we would be broke. If I were leading the parade, we would all be having a blast and enjoying lots of sales, but we'd be running the company by the seat of our pants and jumping on every shiny opportunity that came along. The magic is in the balance, and this confluence of diverse talents is the reason it works . . . and it works exceptionally well. Look at us: the very definition of synergy.

But this isn't how we began. I didn't even know Jim before we started the company and neither of us knew Meredith. The first time I met Jim, it was for breakfast at Bob Evans, hoping that he would point me toward a good candidate for this open position at the newly formed Open Systems Technologies (OST.) Little did I know that Jim would call me later that day with an interest in the job for himself! And here we are, eighteen years later, and we actually still like each other—right, Jim?

About a year after Jim joined me at OST, we both realized how lousy we were at managing projects, which led to our interview with Meredith. I remember two things from our lunch conversation with her that day: one, she had no technology experience, and two, her long-term aspiration was to have my job! It didn't take us long after hiring Meredith to realize we had signed on someone truly special—and that she would, indeed, someday run the company.

Jim was a bit of a mystery in those early years. He used lots of big words that we had never heard before. Not only was his vocabulary over the top—Jim could say something in three big words that would take me twenty small ones—but his breadth and depth of information technology knowledge seemed too good to be true. In fact, I initially wondered if Jim was full of it. I mean, c'mon. There was no way anyone could know this much. And I have never been more wrong. I am still blown away by Jim's technical knowledge and even more so at his insightful way of applying it in practical and beneficial ways for our clients.

Something Special

It wasn't too many years before we realized that we had something very special going on. We came to appreciate and leverage each other's strengths and be less critical of our individual weaknesses. I was always scheming—full of exuberance and starry-eyed ideas. Meredith was my counterbalance—operationally minded and practical. Jim was the brilliant technology visionary—directing us where we needed to go next. When all three of us collaborated on ideas, we knew they would fly.

The confidence and trust didn't come overnight, but when it did come, it was energizing. The best feeling in the world is when you can be completely transparent with your business partners and know that they will not use it against you. Knowing that they will be there for you, no matter what. That is how I feel about Meredith and Jim; I can just be myself and not worry about needing to perform to someone else's standards. I believe that deep down everyone harbors some level of insecurity and yearns for acceptance—and our team gives each other that unconditional acceptance. I look back now, eighteen years later, and realize how blessed I have been to team up with Jim and Meredith.

So what is it—in addition to trust, complementary skill sets, and confidence in each other—that makes it work? I believe it's our total commitment to our company culture and our people. It's also our transparency, willingness to work at our relationships and address the difficult and often uncomfortable stuff that most people avoid.

Adding the Right Leadership People

As our company grew we needed to add people to the leadership team. Theodore Roosevelt was quoted as saying, "The best executive is the one who has sense enough to pick good men to do what he wants done and self-restraint enough to keep from meddling with them while they do it." Over time we did in fact add good leaders and have done our best not to meddle in their day-to-day decision making.

Today there are eight people on the executive team—president/CEO, CIO, director of sales, director of professional services, director of marketing, director of financial operations, chief designer, and executive director. Each time we added another person we had to make sure they were fully committed to our company culture and would be evangelists for OST in all work-related relationships. If not, we would slap them into shape and force them to comply. Just kidding. They needed to model our company culture in their everyday behaviors too. Not kidding.

Now, as new leaders come on board, we teach them what we've learned. The OST way of doing things. Not that the OST way is always best, but it is what's worked to get us to this point of success. We emphasize how much easier it is to lead others when you hire great people and let them do their thing. We also teach our new leaders to give their team members wide, clearly defined boundaries. As long as they stay within these boundaries, they have the freedom to make their own decisions and enjoy a huge degree of flexibility. Obviously, this only works if the employees are self-motivated; if they are not, it doesn't mean they are bad people . . . just not the best fit for OST.

Trust

So we've talked about teaching our new leaders how to serve their people and to give them the freedom to be successful. Another crucial ingredient is trust; there needs to be complete trust between the members of the leadership team and between the leadership team and the people. Without trust, servant leadership and wide boundaries do not work.

As Brian Tracy once said, "The glue that holds all relationships together—including the relationship between the leader and the led—is trust, and trust is based on integrity." What's funny is we don't use the word integrity when describing our company, because we live it. But Brian Tracy is right, integrity and trust are inseparable bedfellows. And trust is integral to every company's success.

I once had someone tell me, "You need to pay more attention to people's hidden agendas." Call me an idealist, but hidden agendas should be banned at every company and within every relationship. They only complicate the already hard work taking placing within any team, company, or organization.

So how to combat those ugly hidden agendas and build trust? I'm convinced that it must be foundational. For instance, every Monday our leadership team gets together for an hour and a half. The first thing we do is go around the room and everyone is required to talk about one "good thing" going on at OST. There are no passes. This sets the tone for the entire meeting. Then we work through that week's agenda of topics—anyone can add a topic. Some are lighthearted and fun to talk about, and others are difficult and stressful to discuss. The difficult topics are the ones that help us to build trust.

These are intense meetings and can get somewhat emotional, partially because our leaders care deeply about the company and its people. The secret to their success is transparency and trust. Once the meeting wraps up we remain committed to one another's success. These weekly meetings have been the single most powerful vehicle for building trust amongst the leadership team. I'm not a huge meeting fan, ask anyone, but I would highly recommend weekly leadership sessions like this for every company no matter how big or how small.

The bottom line—it all comes down to trust.

So What Does This Mean to You?

Does your leadership team have complementary skill sets? If not, consider filling any skill gaps the next time you add or replace a leadership team member.

Does your leadership team have complete trust in each other? Are you transparent with each other? Do you care about each other? Do you all have your eyes on the same prize?

Or do you sense negative tension within your leadership team? Are your people in disagreement over petty situations? Is there competition instead of collaboration? Are they putting themselves first before the team?

You know the answers to these questions and so do your employees and likely those that come into contact with your company. A solid leadership team is the foundation that your company culture is built on.

Not only do you need to trust every member completely, they need to trust each other completely. If your team needs shoring up, do it now; this is the first step in building a business culture you can be proud of.

3

I've Got Your Back

How to Effectively Lead in an Employee-First Culture

CHAPTER THEME SONG:
"I'LL BE THERE," JACKSON FIVE

Riley and Emily Portie died when a drunk driver struck their motorcycle in Orange, Texas, leaving their five children orphaned. Police officer Eric Ellison was one of the first to respond to the terrible crash and was tasked with informing the couple's next of kin of the horrible news.

Their youngest son, Kazzie, was home alone when Ellison arrived at the house to tell him that his parents were dead. When the eighteen-year-old told the kindhearted cop his graduation was just days away and he didn't know what to do, the officer told him he would be there to support him. He explained: "I said, 'You are going to walk! Your mom and dad will have front-row seats looking down from heaven, and I'll stand in their place. I've got your back.'"

The police officer showed up at his graduation ceremony days later. The veteran police officer said the accident and Kazzie struck a chord with him, especially as his own daughter had just graduated recently. He said being there for Kazzie was "the right thing to do."[1]

---

1 Claire Healy, "'I've Got Your Back': Policeman Who Told Teen His Parents Were Killed by Drunk Driver Attends Graduation Ceremony," *Mirror*, June 1, 2015, https://www.mirror.co.uk/news/world-news/ive-your-back-policeman-who-5804146.

"I've got your back" is a phrase that we use often in OST's employee-first culture. Think about it; isn't it essentially what we are all looking for. If a police officer in Orange, Texas, can show up for the graduation of someone who is hurting in the community, surely we can be there for each other at work.

Office Manager Exemplifies Leadership

"Humility is royalty without a crown." —SPENCER W. KIMBALL

If you were to visit OST today, you'd be greeted as you walked through the door by Lisa, our office manager. She'd smile and make you feel welcome. She'd hang your coat up and offer you something to drink. You might be lucky enough to smell freshly baked cookies on the rack by the oven . . . and then try one!

Lisa is an OST legend. She greets every visitor who comes to OST, knows everyone's name, cleans up after us, helps everyone feel welcome, and generally makes the rest of us look like we know nothing about servant leadership. At the center of this success story is surely Lisa's kind heart, but virtually nonexistent boundaries have given her the freedom to flourish. She has taken charge and developed a role that might be some stereotypical cookie-cutter position in another company and made it invaluable to our business.

We are so thankful to have Lisa and can't imagine OST without her. So we take care of her, like we do our other employees. We make sure she can take Fridays off during the summer. We honor her for the grace she shows all of us and give her the latitude to do her job the way she thinks it should be done. She could easily take advantage of all the leeway afforded her, but she doesn't. Instead, she just finds new ways to care for us and help make our office run efficiently.

The kind of servant leadership Lisa and others model at OST is more easily taught by example than explanation. Serving others while keeping their interests ahead of your own runs counter to human nature. It certainly does for me. I naturally consider my own needs before I think of others, so I have to work at helping others succeed without looking for anything in return. We have found that every new leader we add to our mix has a big lesson to learn. They need to be weaned from most everything they've been taught in corporate America. They all love the idealistic concept of being a servant leader, but I guarantee you it is easier said than done.

What Makes a Great Leader?

The first responsibility of a leader is to define reality. The last is to say thank you. In between, the leader is a servant. —MAX DEPREE

Everybody loves a great leader. Even the CEOs of the largest companies in the world want the presidents of their countries, the pastors of their churches, and the principals of their children's schools to be great leaders. And everyone that works at a company wants to be led by a competent team of individuals that can find the right balance between a successful profitable business and caring for the employees. So lead your company—don't leave it to others or think it will happen by itself.

The great debate—are leaders born or developed? The answer—both, but I think that leaders place too much emphasis on their own abilities and not enough emphasis on leveraging the abilities of individuals within their team. Elbert Hubbard said, "It is a fine thing to have ability, but the ability to discover ability in others is the true test." At OST we do our best to uncover the strengths of each individual and leverage them to benefit the individual and the organization. We spend far less time correcting weaknesses.

You don't need a title to be a leader. In my opinion a great leader is a person that everyone can relate to. How often have you heard someone say something like, "Our CEO is awesome, he/she is a really nice person and easy to talk with." It takes a special leader to have the respect of your people, have them like you for who you are, and trust where you are leading them. In a people-first business culture like OST, every leader needs to possess these qualities.

Ultimately employees need to know that you have their back. That means that you will be there for them when they are struggling at work or at home, it means that you will allow them to take chances without the fear of destructive criticism and that you truly believe in them and will defend them when they are right and pick them up when they are wrong.

The Upside Down Pyramid

General George Patton once said, "Lead me, follow me, or get out of my way." This is the antithesis of the OST style of leadership!

The best way to describe our company organization chart is an upside-down pyramid. *Whoa*, you might be thinking, *that defies convention and gravity—and the guy at the bottom would get crushed.* Yep, that guy at the bottom would be me—sitting directly underneath the pointy end. Occasionally painful, granted, but here's how it works: The people that do the real work, the many, are at the top of the pyramid, and the people that are serving them and paving the way to make it easier for them to do their jobs, the few, are at the bottom. It's sort of a reverse trickle-down management style, if you will.

The leadership team at OST exists to serve our customers, company shareholders, and ultimately our employees. But our leaders are no more important—or less—than our team members in operations, technical, and sales. We all work together as peers to accomplish the same goals and objectives.

I realize this servant-leader model is nothing new; these days everyone seems to be jumping on the nontraditional bandwagon. It's easy to say you are a servant leader, but what does it really mean? First and foremost, it says that the company leaders are on your side; and you guessed it—they've got your back. That means you can be yourself, focus on what you are good at, breathe easy, and enjoy your job. It also means the leadership team does everything they can to encourage you, give you challenging opportunities, and help you to grow personally and professionally.

At OST upside down is right side up. Most of us have worked for companies where the leadership posts were synonymous with power positions and often misdirected power at that. At OST, we value leadership no more than the other positions in the company. Many leaders naturally feel that they bring more to the organization compared to other positions; which is probably why it is easier to find managers than it is to find skilled positions like .NET developers. The best leaders know the top of the upside-down pyramid is where the lion's share of the real work gets done.

So What Does This Mean to You?

Ask yourself these questions. Do your employees speak highly of the company and the way it is run? Do your employees treat each other with respect? Are your employees' strengths being leveraged? Do your employees feel like you are there to serve them and help them to be individually successful? Does everyone in your company feel that multiple people have their back? Yep, the answers to all these questions are your responsibility and are dependent on great leadership. If you answered no to some or all of these questions, you should consider making significant changes in the way your company is being lead—consider starting with the upside-down pyramid approach to leadership.

Taller When We Bow

The Place of Humility in a Thriving Organization

CHAPTER THEME SONG:
"IT'S HARD TO BE A SAINT IN THE CITY," BRUCE SPRINGSTEEN

It was a dark and stormy night.

CREWMEMBER: "Captain, Captain, wake up."

CAPTAIN: "Well?"

CREWMEMBER: "Sorry to wake you, sir, but we have a serious problem."

CAPTAIN: "Well, what is it?"

CREWMEMBER: "There's a ship in our sea lane about twenty miles away, and they refuse to move."

CAPTAIN: "What do you mean they refuse to move? Just tell them to move."

CREWMEMBER: "Sir, we have told them; they will not move."

CAPTAIN: "I'll tell them."

THE SIGNAL GOES OUT: "Move starboard 20 degrees."

THE SIGNAL RETURNS: "Move starboard yourself 20 degrees."

CAPTAIN: "I can't believe this. Well, I mean I'm a captain. Let them know who I am. I'm important."

SIGNAL GOES OUT: "This is Captain Horatio Hornblower XXVI, commanding you to move starboard 20 degrees at once."

SIGNAL RETURNS: "This is Seaman Carl Jones II, commanding you to move starboard 20 degrees at once."

CAPTAIN: "What arrogance? I mean, what presumption? Here is a seaman commanding me, a captain. We could just blow them right out of the water. We could just let them know who we are."

SIGNAL: "This is the Mighty Missouri, flag ship of the 7th fleet."

THE SIGNAL RETURNS: "This is the lighthouse."

If humility and respect are to become a cultural dynamic in an organization, these character traits must first be evident in the company's leaders. The way bosses, team leaders, and managers treat each other is how their team members will treat each other. When leaders demonstrate they are there to serve and not to rule or advance their own careers, it speaks volumes about the kind of culture you have.

This can happen in multiple ways. A couple times a year our leadership team makes breakfast for our entire company, then washes the dishes and cleans up afterward. You can see it in the way an employee scrapes the ice off a coworker's car when they're working late, without taking credit. It's there as Lisa Myers and Matt Pince, two amazing OST office managers, greet everyone as they arrive in the morning and check in with them throughout the day. You see it when team members attend the funeral of another team member's relative, even when it means missing an important work meeting.

That Time I Got It Wrong

If this all sounds like Pollyanna's rose-colored HR manual, let me share what happens when the crap hits the fan at OST, which is always the true test of a culture's health and resilience. Jim Vander-Mey, our Chief Innovation Officer, and I were once having a discussion in Jim's office. It started off polite enough; Jim was working on a project that was overdue and I was stressing the vital urgency of getting this project completed.

Jim and I had worked together for many years and knew how

to push each other's buttons. Our words flew back and forth, and our tempers flared into a wildfire neither of us expected or could contain. To make his point, Jim slammed his fist so hard on his desk that I thought he might have broken his hand. As I stormed out of his office, honestly, I hoped he had.

I'm not a fly-off-the-handle anger management candidate most of the time. It's not my temperament, and it's not my leadership style. As I stormed out of Jim's office, I happened to glance over at Tracy, a new employee, who looked startled, hurt, and confused. Getting caught in the cross fire between the CEO and CIO was not what she had bargained for. And she was right to be freaked out. She'd heard all about the great, healthy culture we have at OST, yet the display she witnessed was far from it.

Jim and I needed a few minutes to cool down and think about what had just happened. It didn't take long before we both felt horrible. Not only did we hurt each other, we also hurt Tracy and anyone else playing audience to our inappropriate behavior.

Later in the day Jim and I came together to talk again. Granted, it was a little awkward at first. No one wants to be the first to acknowledge they were out of line. But we apologized to each other and expressed how awful we felt about the whole thing.

Then we walked over to Tracy, explained what had happened, expressed how sorry we were that she had to experience our temper tantrum, and asked for her forgiveness. Our conversation with her was just as important as the one we had with each other. I later found out that we had upset Tracy even more than we realized. She had turned to another OST employee for some consolation and an explanation about the atmosphere in the office that day.

That night when Jim was driving home, he called me, and we talked about the business and how excited we were about our progress. The storm had passed, and we were back to normal. When the next day came, I was as excited to see Jim as he was to see me. I didn't hold a grudge and neither did he because we had taken the time to work through it and put it behind us.

To this day we ask employees not to bury their feelings. If they are upset with someone, we ask them to confront that person about it in a courteous way (the way Jim and I failed to do that one day). After they have expressed their feelings, we encourage them to check with the other person(s) to make sure their relationship is where it needs to be. We're only human and it's easy to put ourselves and our interests first. But an ego-driven focus on competition and office politics destroys the trust, loyalty, and integrity that we take seriously and are committed to practicing daily.

Without humility in the DNA of the culture, pride will metastasize into distrust, deception, and the decline of the business.

That Other Time I Got It Wrong

We all make mistakes, it's true, but sometimes I really am the worst. The other day, I started down the path toward making a big one that would have fundamentally violated our culture at OST. I decided to aggressively recruit several employees from one of our competitors and let people in our office know it. Don't get me wrong, there is nothing wrong with recruiting an individual away from a competitor, but in this case, I was targeting an entire company because I was mad. Thankfully, one of my peers called me out on it, which resulted in a positive change of direction.

No one especially likes to admit when they're wrong, but I knew I had to clear the air and use my mistake as a teaching point for myself and others. From my experience, writing an apology note does wonders to hold the guilty party accountable and help prevent the person who wrote it from repeating the same mistake. So I sent out the following email to the ten people involved in our recruitment conversation:

TO: Recruitment Group
SUBJECT: Recruitment Conversation

"Mike was aware that I was giving the green light to target our competitor as a place for us to recruit talent. Mike challenged

me, saying that this did not feel right to him and that it was
certainly not like me or OST to do something like this; it felt a little
like being a bully."

The more I thought about it, I realized I was upset about how
our competitor was allegedly treating their people but was spinning it in a way that we could gain from it. I recognized that I was
wrong; I was jumping to conclusions about our competitor based
on hearsay and was acting more on emotion than using good business sense. Recruiting an individual is one thing, but the idea of
targeting an entire company does not fit with the way OST does
business. I would certainly not want someone to target OST.

> **TO**: Mike
> **SUBJECT**: Recruitment Conversation
>
> "Mike, thank you for holding me accountable. We have a long
> history at OST of speaking up when something doesn't feel right,
> and I want to encourage everyone at OST to let me or anyone
> else know when we are doing something that doesn't feel right
> or goes against the grain of who we are."

I figure if I'm not willing to eat some humble pie, how can I expect
the people I'm leading to do the same when they make a mistake?
My identity as a leader must be based on my strength of character
as a human being, not on trying to look perfect and getting defensive when I'm not. Humility is not thinking less of yourself than
others. It's being genuine with yourself alongside others.

How to Get Ahead

Business cultures built on humility and genuine attitudes of respect
tend to thrive while those founded on top-down autocratic behaviors are likely to stall over the long haul. If you need everyone to
recognize how powerful, brilliant, and authoritative you are, you'll
never win the loyalty of the people you lead. Humility inspires

trust, which in turn forges a bond of loyalty. It's foundational for a healthy business culture.

Maybe you're thinking, "I hear you, Dan, but you don't know what it's like where I work. It's cutthroat! No one has my back, so sometimes I have to step on a few people to get ahead. It's great for you to talk about humility because you're a successful CEO. But in the real world you've got to put yourself first." If this is your priority—putting yourself first—you'll never achieve your goal of getting ahead. That's a promise. It's the irony of arrogance. Oh, playing hardball at the expense of others may work for a while, but eventually you'll reach a plateau because no one will trust you.

People often ask us, "Don't people take advantage of you with this kind of culture?" Our answer is usually something like, "Yes, sometimes people do take advantage of our culture—but the positives of living and working this way far outweigh the negatives." In the long run we're all better off.

So What Does This Mean to You?

Humility is more than being modest. If you are a leader in your organization, owning up to things in a humble way sets the tone for everyone else. If you lose your patience with someone and exercise your authority in an inappropriate way, make sure to apologize to the individual(s) in a timely manner. If you make a mistake admit that you were wrong. Saying the words, "I'm sorry, I was wrong," can be cleansing for yourself and refreshing for others.

Never take yourself too seriously, strive to be a giver instead of a taker, tell people what you are thinking without hidden agendas, and get used to being vulnerable. No matter what your role is in a company, your attitude of humility will become contagious.

How Much Is Enough

An "It's Important, Just Not Too Important" Approach to Profit

CHAPTER THEME SONG:
"MONEY," PINK FLOYD

While I often can't recall what I had for dinner last night, I'll never forget the name Jakob Fugger from business school at Michigan State University. According to my professor, Jakob was the businessman to coin the phrase "business is business." In other words, if you lose and I win, "Hey, business is business." On a whim I decided to find out who this Jakob Fugger character was. Anyone with a name like his is bound to have a colorful story.

It turns out Jakob Fugger (1459 to 1525) was one of the richest men ever to walk the earth. In today's dollars, he was worth more than $250 *billion*. That's more than four times Bill Gates net worth. Born in Germany, Fugger was the son of a textile businessman, and he gained his wealth in the banking, mining, and metal trade industries doing business with the likes of Maximilian I (Holy Roman Emperor) and the Vatican.

Martin Luther's observation that "Fugger and similar people really need to be kept in check" leads me to think Fugger was an aggressive businessman, the Donald Trump of his day. When he died Jakob Fugger was the richest man in the world, which explains why he's referred to as "Jakob Fugger the Rich" in the history books.

At the end of the day, business is nothing more than buying low and selling high, and OST is no different from any other business in this regard. We need profits, so we can pay our people well and support our entrepreneurial culture. But at OST the idea that "business is business" is not the way we operate. We make decisions based on our employees and their families first and our customers second. We trust profits to fall in place as a result, and they have.

We would revise Fugger's best-known phrase to "business is people." Without compassion, caring, and community, all you have left is a bunch of numbers as a footnote in a history book. At most companies, profit trumps everything. At OST, company culture trumps everything!

How We Increased Profit (But Not Too Much)

Like any sustainable business enterprise, OST needs profit to operate. An engine is useless without a power source, the human body can't survive without air, and OST is nonexistent without profit. Nothing is inherently unique about this, but the way we make decisions about profitability is.

How much profit is enough? If you ask the Jakob Fuggers of the world, they would likely scoff at such a question. In some ways I laugh at the question myself because I don't know a businessperson alive who would not enjoy making more profit, including me. But when profit is the sole priority, many companies end up undermining their greatest resource—their people and company culture. Whether you dismiss OST's philosophy as idealistic or find it a refreshing inspiration (I hope the latter), our people-first model has certainly served us well. We've been profitable in forty-two of our last forty-four quarters, which means we've made a profit over 95 percent of the time we've been in business.

Part of the difference in our perspective on profit involves viewing it as a means to an end, not the end itself. Primarily we need to be profitable to nourish our culture and facilitate an environment where work-life balance, employee professional growth, and entrepreneurial opportunities exist for everyone. Since OST is partially owned by our employees (more about this soon) and most of our people have some form of incentive compensation, profit motivates and rewards everyone's drive toward success.

It is easy to become greedy, so we must remain vigilant about finding the optimal balance between culture and profitability. A few years back our net-profit-to-revenue ratio had dipped to 4 percent. An acceptable level for some, but this ratio didn't allow us enough freedom to invest in the future, and we knew the economy would not stay strong forever, so we needed a buffer.

In our industry "best in class" profitability ranges from 10 to 12 percent. We were not concerned about how we measured up to best in class companies because our culture of giving would not necessarily support this level of profitability quarter to quarter, year to year. But we needed to increase our profitability to a healthy level to protect our employees' jobs and invest in the future. We knew if we really wanted to sustain growth for years and decades to come, we had to make some short-term adjustments. So after months of discussion and financial analysis, we chose 5.5 percent as the minimum threshold of profitability for OST moving forward and 6 percent as the target. There's no magic formula, and this number will vary for every company and from industry to industry. But if you make supporting a healthy culture the priority for the long term, you can find the right margin for the specific needs of your business.

The difference between 4 percent and 5.5 percent doesn't sound like much, but closing this gap was a major undertaking for OST. We either had to increase our prices to our clients, cut costs, or a combination of both. At the time we did not feel we could increase prices, so we pursued cutting costs. From start to finish it took us about six months to make the final decisions on which areas to trim. Along the way we kept reminding ourselves that the decision to cut costs was in the best interests of everyone—not just leaders or shareholders (in our case, the shareholders are the employees.) This motivated us to keep doing something that was at times unpleasant. We continually held each other accountable to make sure we were not letting our personal motivations, biases, or greed get in the way of making fair decisions.

The lion's share of the cost cutting was in two areas: (1) salesperson commissions and (2) healthcare benefits. We had known for a long time our sales commission rates were tops in the industry, and if we enjoyed healthy profitability this was fine. While our proposed change would hit our sales people hard, their new commission rate would still be in the top 10 percent for our industry. Regarding healthcare, OST had always paid for 100 percent of our employee benefits. We were proud of this, but with costs rising in double digits annually, we needed our employees to contribute a portion of this cost. Our analysis showed that making these changes would bring us to a net profit of approximately 6.1 percent.

How They Took It

The hardest part was announcing the cost cuts to our employees. We didn't know how they would take the largest cost reduction we had ever made as a company. How we chose to communicate the news would be crucial, so we decided to host a company-wide conference call, allowing everyone to learn of the cuts simultaneously. The theme of the call was all about healthy profitability—maintaining our culture of keeping people first and retaining the funds to fuel growth. I explained how best in class profitability was normally between 10 and 12 percent in our industry, and why we found a much lower 6 percent to be sufficient for OST. We didn't feel we were asking too much. The bottom line was that we needed this level of profitability to maintain our valued culture.

The individual responses from our employees, both directly as well as what we could pick up around the water cooler, was surprisingly positive. Our employees didn't like the cuts. Who would? But it was clear they trusted us and understood we needed to be proactive. Our employees' positive responses were reinforced by the results of an employee survey a month later. We had expected a temporary dive in these scores compared to past surveys—after all, we had just dropped a financial bomb on our team members. Astonishingly, the survey results were in line with those of six months earlier and extremely positive. I attribute weathering this potential setback to thorough planning, thoughtfulness in approach, and a culture of trust.

Other Profitability Strategies

For Jakob Fugger and his corporate disciples in the twenty-first century, business amounts to nothing more than buying low and selling high. However, when it comes to profitability, many more factors and variables must be included in a smart strategy. At OST we have always focused on making short-term decisions that match up with our long-term vision. This balanced thinking helps us keep profitability in its rightful place without elevating it as the only goal.

Other strategies we've used to keep our profits healthy include keeping debt to a minimum, being fiscally conservative, and reinvesting a reasonable amount of our profit back into the company to reduce cash flow pressure and leave enough money liquid for growth. We are also slow to hire unless we know the income generated from the new person exceeds our costs. This is relatively easy to do for a sales person or billable resource, but more difficult for new overhead positions like members of the leadership team.

When our company was small we all wore multiple hats. I was general manager, sales manager, president, sales person, custodian, chief cook, and bottle washer—and that's just before lunch. As we grew it was difficult to delegate responsibilities primarily because there was no one to delegate to. The idea of bringing on new people to take on some of our responsibilities was overwhelming, especially because we didn't feel we had enough money to fund them and still make a healthy profit. So these decisions were delayed, ignored, disregarded, delayed, and generally deferred. If you've ever helped launch a start-up, I'm sure you can relate.

Having input from a trusted consultant at the right time helped us. A turning point for OST was a meeting in 2007 with Pat Barbour, a trusted banker and friend. Pat understood our business and had supported us since our inception. We included Pat in the meeting because we respected his business judgment, needed outside council, and knew he had our best interests in mind.

The meeting was straightforward but powerful. Meredith, Jim, and I often refer to this as a transformational meeting for OST and for us personally. Pat asked us each to write our names on a whiteboard along with a list of individual responsibilities—in other words, where we spent our time. Then he had us circle the responsibilities only we could do. These were responsibilities that would negatively affect the company if someone else did them, the ones where we added the most value to the organization. This, of course, left a list of responsibilities that could be transferred to someone else in the company or to a new person if that made sense. Pat went a step further and asked us to challenge each other to see if we had circled items that were actually transferable.

I'll never forget the outcome of the meeting. Pat told us we needed to hire a sales manager and an accountant. He said we were about two years late on hiring the sales manager, but this wasn't all bad. In his experience, which was abundant, companies that waited as long as possible to hire new overhead positions were much more likely to succeed. This conservative approach helped assure profitability even during high growth periods.

Business cultures that promote excessive spending and risk taking beyond what they can afford to lose may flourish for a period, but never for the long haul. Building and maintaining a profitable company is a well-planned marathon, not a greedy sprint.

Scotty's Money Machine

On a lighter note, a long time ago when the fax machine was king, one of our sales reps, Scott Dare, received software orders daily via fax. Scotty is still with OST today. Whenever the fax machine fired up, we all would race to see how big the order was. Sometimes it would run for a minute straight spitting out orders. This continued for months, and Scotty was loving it. So was the company.

After the second month I had a brass plate engraved with the words "Scotty's Money Machine" and stuck it above the fax machine. Everyone had a good laugh, including Scotty. Just because we put our employees, families, and clients before profitability doesn't mean we don't enjoy the excitement of a sale!

We try to have fun with everything we do at OST, and that includes profitability.

So What Does This Mean to You?

I often ask business owners, "Why are you in business?" All too often I get the answer, "To make money." Wrong answer! If you are just in business to make money, you might be lucky enough to make a little over the short term, but anything lasting is unlikely.

What is it about your business that you are most passionate about? If you focus on your passion, the financial success will eventually come. If you are having trouble coming up what you are all about, focus on taking care of your people like OST does—it's a no-brainer. You inherently need profit to thrive as a business, but it should never be the reason that you are in business.

······················· (6) ·······························

Grow, Baby, Grow

Responsible Expansion in a Fast-Changing World

CHAPTER THEME SONG:
"IT'S BEEN A LOVELY CRUISE," JIMMY BUFFET

About ten years ago, the year after we completed the employee buyout of OST, we decided to hire a consultant to see how we measured up to our peers in the industry. The consultant was from a Midwest accounting and professional services firm that used a methodology called Balanced Scorecard. He surveyed all of our employees and found that we were number two out of the twenty-five companies that he had worked with when it came to morale.

We were surprised that we were not number one, but number two was not all bad. When the consultant asked us what our revenue growth goals were for the next three to five years, we responded, "If we can maintain our revenue at the same level as it is right now, we'll be happy." Then the consultant inquired about our net profit targets over the coming years. When we answered his question with the same answer, he was incredulous: "OST is the only company out of twenty-five that is not interested in growing their revenue and profitability!"

Well, since he put it that way! Without changing anything we were doing, from that point on we grew like wildfire. As a matter of fact, we grew our revenue by over thirty percent compounded annually for eleven years. From $5 million in annual revenue in 2003 to $160 million in 2014. The growth started spontaneously; it wasn't our intentional goal. But apparently we were doing something right for our clients.

A few years later we realized that we liked the growth and started to embrace it; not only did it provide the opportunity for additional income, but it also brought new and exciting ideas into the company. Since then, we've actually focused on growth to infuse energy into OST—never growing for the mere sake of getting bigger.

Sensing a Need for Stabilization

One way we protect our culture during periods of fast growth is something we call "stabilization mode." Every so often when a company grows too quickly, people begin to feel overwhelmed and need a breather. This has happened at least five times over the past eleven years at OST. The idea is to put a freeze on new initiatives as much as possible and concentrate on the ones we have. We also slow down on hiring new people to keep change and disruption to a minimum. These stabilization periods typically last between six and twelve months and are a welcome change for most.

Determining when to declare a stabilization mode can be tough, but there are signs. People start working considerably longer hours than usual, and all of the sudden they're grouchy (surprise). Customer complaints increase, margins decline, data from staff surveys head south, and a general feeling of chaos begins to take over the place. In most cases, when I've suggested we go into stabilization mode, it's been one of those intuitive decisions made on a gut level. The same is true when the decision comes to get back on the fast track. I've tried to be attuned to how our employees are feeling when making these decisions.

Periods of stabilization have brought many benefits. They've allowed us and our new employees time to get to know each other, time to plan, time to shore up and invest in our existing business initiatives, time to refine our business processes, time to focus on increasing OST services utilization, revenue, and profitability, and most importantly, time to nurture our culture. I strongly recommend that fast-growing companies consider purposeful stabilization periods as a means of maintaining and nurturing a healthy culture.

Reinvention

Taking time to breathe is essential and the slack times they create are great for analyzing where you fit into your industry and what you need to do stay a step ahead. Another part of our company's success and an integral part of our vibrant culture has been our willingness to continually reinvent ourselves. Companies require flexibility to stay vibrant, relevant, and create new employee opportunities for growth from within. We've seen companies that don't embrace this kind of change; they become stagnant and often lose their edge. In the information technology marketplace, if you are unwilling to change, you go out of business—mega fast. With the exception of monopolies, this is probably true in every industry. Consider the incredible pace of change in consumer optical video recording technology: VHS, CD, DVD, Blu-ray, and online services like Netflix and Amazon—all in a period of about forty years.

Reinvention is key to driving organic growth within a business. But regardless of your growth strategy, constant change and keeping current is vital to company health.

This or That Kind of Growth

Experts will tell you the easiest way to accelerate growth is to buy another company. I don't have a strong preference when it comes to organic growth versus growth through acquisition. Everyone agrees, however, that determining cultural compatibility between companies is one of the most important criteria when expanding through acquisition. Simply put, if the culture is not compatible, put away your checkbook, stay away from the bank loan officer, and chill.

All of our growth has been organic with the exception of two acquisitions. But those purchases turned out to be some of the best decisions we ever made. Cultural compatibility and values were paramount, or we would not have moved ahead with the deals. They both turned out to be natural fits, allowing us to add new services that would have been almost impossible to learn organically.

In the future we plan to continue double-digit growth as the market allows. We believe we can accomplish this organically, but we will not hesitate to consider acquisitions. On balance, acquiring a company is a legitimate expansion strategy, but should never become your only means of growth.

Growing Responsibly

Growth is great, but it begs the question, "Will growing too fast threaten our culture?" This remains a major concern at OST. We worry about the disruption and consternation caused by fast-paced change—issues like employee burnout, poor customer service, dwindling profits, insufficient processes, and the problems caused by waiting too long to hire. We also worry about growing too big and losing the entrepreneurial, small-company feel that most people crave.

We have experienced profound growing pains at several revenue hurdles—such as $5 million, $10 million, $20 million, $50 million, and $100 million. This is not uncommon for fast-growing companies. As a matter of fact, every business leader I'm aware of who navigated a company over these hurdles can relate. Every year we need to make significant changes in how we run the business in order to accommodate change. This allows us to grow steadily while maintaining our culture and client satisfaction.

A few years back when we were a $55 million-dollar company, we had five people on the leadership team overseeing seventeen business initiatives. The good news was that all five people on the leadership team knew everything that was going on in all seventeen initiatives. The bad news was that all five people on the leadership team knew everything that was going on in all seventeen initiatives. This way of doing business worked when we had three leadership people and six business initiatives, but it was becoming increasingly unmanageable. We realized we had hit another revenue hurdle and needed to switch up our business model. Fortunately, the flexibility to do this efficiently and effectively was built in to our company's culture.

Some of the larger issues we were facing included a lack of focus, lack of business initiative accountability, lack of consolidated goals for each business initiative, and several underperforming business initiatives. Put simply, there were just too many initiatives, and limited ownership behind them.

In order to overcome these issues, we decided to break the business initiatives into manageable "chunks." We ended up reducing the number of initiatives from seventeen to twelve. We also introduced a new accountability structure aligning each business initiative with one business owner and one executive sponsor. The business owners and executive sponsors then created a two- to three-page mini business plan and were held accountable to their progress on actions and goals in quarterly meetings.

The benefits of this new methodology have included better focus, easier-to-manage and significantly increased accountability, consistent consolidated goals, leveraged leadership strengths, and fewer underperforming business initiatives. It has literally made a world of difference as evidenced by the fact that we are still refining and using this process today.

Other examples of changes we have made at various stages of our growth include the addition of a project management office, a new statement of work process, a client satisfaction survey sent out after every services engagement, an employee satisfaction survey sent out every six months, and a company dashboard shared with everyone in the company. In other words, clear communication, transparency, accountability, and then more clear communication. Regardless of how you monitor and measure these qualities, you must use them as a barometer for your culture in the midst of growth spurts.

The key to sustaining healthy growth in any company is making sure your culture keeps pace and adapts to your growth. Be willing to slow down if folks need time to catch up.

How Big Is Too Big?

At OST we're concerned about pace of growth, we're also concerned about growing too big. Ironically, I feel that our culture has improved in many ways as we have grown. For example, the opportunities for advancement at OST are enormous compared to what they were ten years ago. The opportunity to be an entrepreneur at OST and start up a "business within a business" is a direct result of our growth. Some people still long for the "good old days" when we were only ten to twenty people, but it is impossible to recreate that culture. We must embrace the company we are today.

With this truth in mind, we continually consider new business initiatives in the process of reinventing ourselves. This is consistent with our culture of entrepreneurship. New business opportunities present themselves on a regular basis at OST. The key to success is sorting through the hundreds of possibilities and choosing those that are congruent with our core business, indicate the highest probability of success, and have the potential for strengthening our overall business. We try to keep a balanced perspective, knowing that most of our new business initiatives will either be mildly successful or fail.

Perseverance pays off when it comes to organic growth through new initiatives. If you keep at it long enough, eventually you will unearth some big successes. However, for every big success there will likely be multiple failures, so employees need to know it is safe to take risks . . . and okay to fail. The leadership team, in turn, needs to know how to pick employees up, support, and encourage them when these inevitable failures occur. This entrepreneurial-focused mindset needs to be deeply engrained in your culture to succeed. Bottom line: the positive benefits of growth far outweigh the risks if your company remains focused on maintaining, cultivating, and improving your culture throughout the growth process.

So What Does This Mean to You?

Have you been growing at a fast pace and experiencing problems as a result? If so, don't be afraid to slow it down for a brief period to let people catch their breath. Growing too fast is a great problem to have if handled properly. Embrace your growth and capitalize on the energy and new opportunities that it creates for everyone.

Or is your company growing slowly, holding steady, or even shrinking? If so, your company may be feeling stagnant and the morale could probably use a boost. Think about introducing a new product or service. Consider making positive changes in your sales organization or expanding into a new territory. Find new ways to invigorate your employees. (There are lots of ideas throughout the remainder of this book.)

Growth for growth sake never works, but if you are growing because your clients love your products or services, because you are acquiring culturally compatible companies, because you are expanding into new geographies, or because you are introducing new products or services, grow, baby, grow and enjoy the ride!

The Silver Bullet

Why Every Company Should Think Seriously about Employee Ownership

CHAPTER THEME SONG:
"SWEET CHILD O' MINE," GUNS N' ROSES

The Road Not Taken

Two roads diverged in a yellow wood,
And sorry I could not travel both
And be one traveler, long I stood
And looked down one as far as I could
To where it bent in the undergrowth;

Then took the other, as just as fair,
And having perhaps the better claim,
Because it was grassy and wanted wear;
Though as for that the passing there
Had worn them really about the same,

And both that morning equally lay
In leaves no step had trodden black.
Oh, I kept the first for another day!
Yet knowing how way leads on to way,
I doubted if I should ever come back.

I shall be telling this with a sigh
Somewhere ages and ages hence:
Two roads diverged in a wood, and I—
I took the one less traveled by,
And that has made all the difference.
—ROBERT FROST

Employee ownership makes up less than 15 percent of the private sector workforce; yet it is the ultimate perk. Consider taking the road less traveled.

If I had to name one foundational ingredient, the proverbial "silver bullet" for creating a healthy, productive culture in a private company, employee ownership would be it. In the early years of OST, allowing employees to share in both the risks and rewards created a bigger impact than anything else we did to establish a sense of purpose and loyalty. It's easy to provide incentives for your employees and talk about the importance of corporate culture, but employee ownership makes an undeniable statement about the attitude at the top.

If you've ever spoken with someone who owned a portion of the private company employing them, you've seen the gleam of ownership and subtle smile of pride as they described their investment in that business. Regardless of how great or small the shares, employee ownership unifies the company with a sense of shared commitment to success. This kind of investment provides another critical component to help employees feel a part of something bigger than themselves.

Employees benefit because they can see a direct correlation between their efforts and the returns they receive in the form of dividends. This cause-effect awareness gives them purpose and hope for the future. They're thinking, "If we can grow this company tenfold, my two percent ownership will really be worth something."

It is true that providing employees with ownership dilutes the primary owner or owner's shares, but I'm convinced the benefits far outweigh the costs. No matter their number of shares, employees develop an enormous amount of pride, often disproportionate to their level of ownership. Employees are also less likely to leave the company when they own a part of it; this is due partly to loyalty and partly to financial incentives. Larger shareholders may also be hesitant to leave especially if they have seen the company stock values rising. We also leverage ownership as a recruiting tool; even a few shares are a big deal to prospective employees.

Selfishly, I've found employee ownership has made my life much easier over the past dozen years. Running an employee-owned company is like riding a Harley instead of a three-speed bicycle. Forget pedaling. I just steer and hang on!

Creating the Framework

Creating an employee stock ownership plan is not rocket science. It's relatively easy to do, but as with most things the devil is in the details. If you pursue this game-changing initiative, my advice is to work with an experienced corporate attorney and take the time to think through the finer points.

We decided to be an employee-owned organization when we purchased OST from our parent company in 2003. We were too small to afford a traditional Employee Stock Ownership Plan (ESOP) and too naïve to shrink away from creating a custom framework of our own. There were just seven of us in the beginning, but we wanted an employee ownership plan that would grow with us, cover all of our bases, and allow for future employees to buy in.

Our Shareholder Buy and Sell Agreement (SBSA) and Operating Agreement serve as the legal basis for our employee ownership plan at OST. Theoretically it contains every possible scenario regarding stock ownership. For example, the three areas of dividend payout—buying, selling, and pricing the stock—are all included in our SBSA. In addition, it describes what happens if a shareholder leaves the company of their own free will, is terminated from the company, dies, goes bankrupt, is divorced, or has a permanent disability. It also covers topics like life insurance coverage, a covenant not to compete, a right to examine books, and personal guarantees.

To be an effective tool with tangible benefits, the ownership system needed to be real—not like other programs we had seen where employers gave employee ownership with no way to sell and no annual income.

Our highest priority required deciding how much net profit to pay to shareholders each year and how much to keep in the company. We wanted to pay out as much as possible, but we also knew that we had to hold back enough cash to keep it running. The money left in the company would be for general operations, cash flow, and future expansion. At first, we paid 80 to 90 percent of net profits but quickly learned that 70 percent was a more realistic number, and we've been paying out at this rate for several years.

We also considered the timing of the payouts and chose to make them quarterly based on the net profit of the previous three months. While this worked initially, over time we realized this stretched our cash flow a bit thin at times. So we switched to more conservative payments each quarter and made up for any shortfalls at the end of the year. At minimum we paid out enough to cover quarterly income tax estimates. Overall, this approach has served us well.

Spreading the Wealth

Originally OST's seven founding shareholders owned 100 percent of the stock. As the company grew, we needed a simple way for others to purchase stock, which obviously meant we needed available stock to sell. Fortunately, one of our shareholders was willing to sell a portion of his stock to make stock available for our new people. If you are creating an employee ownership program for the first time, I recommend reserving at least 10 percent of the stock right away for future employees to buy in.

Whenever we had available stock, we announced the details

to our employees. These announcements included the price of the stock, a description of how our stock program worked, and an indication of past performance. We did not tell the employees the total amount of stock available; we just asked them if they were interested in purchasing stock, and if so how much.

Every stock offering at OST has been significantly oversubscribed. While this reflects great enthusiasm and confidence in our company, it has required the COO and me to make decisions on how much stock each employee could purchase. Once all the requests were in and we had made the decisions on how many shares each employee would receive, we communicated to each requester individually with how many shares they were authorized to purchase.

Occasionally an employee was disappointed in the number of shares that they could purchase, but for the most part the entire process of offering stock and accepting stock purchases was a positive one.

Determining the Stock Price

One of our leadership team's most important tasks is determining the annual stock price. Initially, it was derived from the purchase price of the company. To make it simple and fair, if someone paid 20 percent of the purchase price, they owned twenty percent of the company.

Going forward we wanted it to work the same way. We would establish a value for the company every year based on the prior year's earnings and the stock price would reflect this company value.

To determine our value, every year we checked with industry experts to find out what the going multiplier was for evaluation purposes. In our industry, company evaluations are typically based on a multiple of EBITDA (Earnings before Interest, Taxes, Depreciation, and Amortization). It's a simple calculation. If the multiple being used is 5, for example, and a company's EBITDA is $2 million, the value of the company is $10 million.

We try to be on the conservative side of the valuation range, because OST is a privately held company with no independent trading mechanism for its stock. We also wanted to guard against an inflated valuation that would encourage employees to sell and possibly leave the company.

Once a year we announce the new company value to all employee owners. In the beginning we expected to get some pushback, but it never came. We were always transparent about how we determined the value using the low end of the industry multiplier with net earnings. The owners have always been comfortable with this approach because it is simple, consistent, fair, and because we have worked hard to build a culture of trust.

Preparing for Different Possibilities

A few years back we sold a large portion of the OST stock to an outside investor. We were only willing to sell if they would leave everything in place, let us keep a significant ownership percentage, and allow us to make 100 percent of the day-to-day decisions.

Selling a portion of the company diluted our stock, but we were still able to maintain ownership in the company. Since then there have been multiple opportunities for employees to purchase stock and the demand continues be high.

At the time of the sale we had a big decision to make. There were five owners holding over three-quarters of the company stock. How would we take care of the dedicated employees who would not benefit from the sale? The solution was simple but would require sacrifice. We agreed to give away 10 percent of the sale to OST employees who did not own stock, the ones who had only a small amount of stock, and those who had made significant contributions to the company's success. While it's never easy giving away large amounts of money, this distribution remains one of the most fulfilling things we've ever done. It was the right thing to do and added fuel to our healthy business culture.

As you can see there's a lot to consider, but you're likely to find the development of an employee ownership plan easier than you first expected. Once you have the program in place, the key to success is continual communication with your employees. If you do not have an employee stock ownership plan in place, it's worth investigating. For us the cultural dividends have far outstripped the fiscal costs.

So What Does This Mean to You?

Let me be clear—if you are a privately held company and do not offer employee ownership you should at least consider it. If you are a publicly held company you should offer stock and stock option purchase incentives.

If you are considering the possibility of going all the way in becoming an employee-owned company, the following questions may help you to get your thinking started in the right direction. What legal structure will you use; a formal ESOP or less formal custom agreement? How many shares will you offer to the general employee population? Will you provide a special offering to the leadership team? How will you determine the price of your stock? How much of your annual earnings will you pay your shareholders as dividends? How often will you pay dividends? How often will you offer shares to your employees? How will you determine how many shares each employee can purchase if the shares are over-subscribed? How will you make sure that there are shares available to employees in the future without diluting your stock value?

These are just a few of the hundreds of questions that need to be answered, but don't let that overwhelm you. We were successful in rolling out our employee ownership program at OST without a hitch. Keep it simple and use common sense. And don't just talk about it—if you are considering an employee ownership program, get started now!

PART TWO

CULTURE TRUMPS EVERYTHING

Caring for Employees

······················⟨ 8 ⟩·····················

Hundred Dollar Bills
and Paper Airplanes

Using Contests and Competitions to Boost Morale and Get Results

CHAPTER THEME SONG:
"YOU RAISE ME UP," JOSH GROBAN

Imagine walking into your workplace on a normal day. As you say your good mornings, grab a coffee, and walk to your workstation, you take a quick peek in your mail slot. You don't really expect to see anything (mail isn't delivered until one o'clock), but . . . wait a second. There's an envelope in there—just a plain white envelope on which someone has handwritten your name. Your curiosity overwhelms you. You rip into it and pull out a hundred dollar bill. You look again and see a note. It's from the CEO: "Thanks for turning that project around so quickly. You're awesome."

How would you feel in that moment?

One of my favorite ways to reinforce a sense of belonging and show appreciation to our employees might surprise you: it's through competitions, contests, and crazy incentives. When everyone participates in a company contest or competition, a bond forms within the culture. If the competition is lighthearted, even silly, everyone has a lot of fun. Adding a legitimate prize makes it worth the effort and incentivizes team members to participate.

Crazy Bucks

"Crazy Bucks" may be a lackluster name, but it was a barn burner of a contest and one of my personal all-time favorites. The beautiful thing about contests, if done right, is they have the potential to achieve multiple benefits with a single event. At OST we use contests as another tool to tune up our culture and increase energy levels and work enjoyment. In the case of Crazy Bucks, the objective was to motivate our employees to increase billable hours as we closed out the calendar year. The contest included everyone in the company, which served the second purpose of boosting an already thriving morale.

Our executive team decided to give away a maximum of $25,000 in hundred dollar bills as a way of making the reward seem tangible and immediate. We knew it was a risk, but the contest would not cost us a cent if we were successful in driving an incremental $25,000 in billable services. Anything beyond $25,000 would be a bonus.

To increase the fun factor, we hammed up the contest announcement with every over-the-top used car salesman cliché and joke we could imagine. Here's the announcement that we sent to our employees:

I've got two words for you—Crazy Bucks! Yep you heard it right—one, Crazy—two, Bucks! Get ready for the biggest Crazy Bucks contest in history (and maybe the only one)! Bonus cash! Nine weeks only! Get ready to be wowed!—Wow! We've got $25,000 in crisp $100 bills that we are hoping to give away!—Wow! Again!—Has Dan gone crazy? Yep! No haggling, no hassles—we need to move these bucks to make room for others coming in!

OST Crazy Bucks Contest Rules
$25,000—everything is literally paid in crisp $100 bills!

EVERYONE ELIGIBLE (135 $100 bills)—If OST bills at our aggressive revenue target in professional services for the months of November and December, every employee and intern at OST gets a $100 bill.

BILLABLE CONSULTANTS ELIGIBLE (45 $100 bills)—Every week, starting the first week of November, the five employees who bill the most hours for that week will each receive a $100 bill. This is a nine-week contest.

EVERYONE ELIGIBLE (70 $100 bills)—Jim VanderMey, Bill Herrington, Dave Gerrity, Dan Behm, John Thayer, Meredith Bronk, and John Vancil will each be given a stack of $100 bills—ten each ($1,000 each.) They will be giving away these $100 bills to reward employees for positive behavior and positive results during the months of November and December. There are no rules for this portion of the contest.

What can you do with your $100 bills? Anything you like! Just think of the possibilities . . . Buy your pooch a grooming appointment. Send your $100 bill to a starving college student. Buy your favorite person a bottle of wine. (I like Silver Oak 2006 Napa Cabernet Sauvignon.) Have Chia Pets delivered to all of your friends. Buy eight pounds of Mackinac Island Fudge. Purchase a vacuum cleaner for your spouse for Christmas. The possibilities are endless!

Silly? Yes. Corny? Uh huh. Effective? Like you wouldn't believe! The Crazy Bucks contest exceeded our expectations and was a smash hit with our employees. As participation gained momentum, I really hammed it up and had way too much fun playing the part of the stereotypical used car salesman. "Dan Dan the Used Car Man" sported dark sunglasses (indoors), a wide-collar shirt unbuttoned enough to show off a thick gold chain, and a big ole (unlit) stogie. I am sure some people thought I really was crazy—and maybe I am.

Dan Dan the Used Car Man

The best part of the contest was handing out hundred dollar bills. A couple of our recruiters had been hosting evening "meet and greet" sessions with prospective employees. Instead of the usual verbal thank you, I showed my appreciation for their efforts with hundred dollar bills. Tad McConkey in our Detroit office told me it was the coolest thing ever, going to his mailbox, opening an envelope, and discovering a crisp hundred dollar bill. There were numerous stories from our leadership team, but I'll leave those to your imagination.

In the end we paid out the entire $25,000. There was no way to know if we generated an additional $25,000 in billable hours as a direct result of the contest, but it felt like our numbers went up at least $100,000 or more. Sales incentives are often part of every company's culture, but why not give it a theme, broaden it beyond the sales team, and have as much fun as possible? Incentives like "Crazy Bucks" don't have to risk much financially to be a hit; you could use one, five, ten, or twenty dollar bills instead of hundred dollar bills and be just as effective.

Paper Airplanes

These kinds of competitions often work best when everyone is committed to solving a problem or achieving a goal together. With Crazy Bucks, it was about increasing billable hours. But here's another situation where we harnessed a competitive contest simply to nourish our company's culture.

A few years ago, we added a paper airplane to our logo to make sure people realized it was a window. We thought adding a paper airplane exiting the window would signify a whimsical, fun-loving

The OST Logo

culture as well as visually clarify the three windowpanes used in the graphic. As we introduced the paper airplane in several new marketing campaigns, it seemed only natural to conduct a company-wide paper airplane–throwing contest.

We felt like little kids planning the event. This was the OST culture in action. The stated objective was to "design, document, fabricate (or fold), and test-fly a 'paper' airplane to demonstrate maximum linear distance of flight." In the weeks leading up to the big event, the recycle bins overflowed with folded paper. Friendly trash talk heated up both individual and departmental rivalries as competitors put on their game faces. The prizes at stake? What else—airline vouchers starting at one thousand dollars!

Here are a few of the contest rules we established and posted:

Prior to the launching, each competitor shall submit their aircraft to the judges for inspection. After verifying that the entry complies with the contest construction specifications, the plane may take flight.

The fly-off will be held in an indoor facility with sufficient floor space and ceiling height and shall consist of a maximum of two valid flights per entry. When your turn arrives, the launcher will retrieve the aircraft from the staging area and launch the plane from the marked area on the floor of the competition area. An official will measure the distance of each flight from release to the moment of first contact with the floor.

If the aircraft flies outside the designated area, and should touch a structure (wall, column, etc.) or spectator during flight, that flight will be declared ended at that moment. If the aircraft touches, is aided by, or interfered with by that entry's owner during flight, that flight will be considered valid, but zero inches will be noted for that flight.

Between flights, the owner may straighten, refold, and/or adjust their aircraft but no new material is to be added (the plane should be sturdy enough to survive a normal flight without needing major repairs). The judges may allow exceptions to this rule in extreme cases, such as for damage caused on purpose by spectator interference.

Including our guidelines on plane specifications and construction, the rules totaled more than three pages. Pretty funny considering we were making paper airplanes! Everyone seemed to have a great time and appreciate our planning and promotional efforts. Most of the company participated in the contest, and it was fun to see the creative contest entries. You would think that one paper airplane would run away with the contest, but it was actually very close. The contest was clearly a cultural winner and showed employees that we care about more than just dollars and cents.

From time to time OST gets to feeling a little too normal, so we dream up another contest. What would your version of the paper airplane contest be for your company? What inexpensive, silly competition would unite everyone's interests and foster unexpected fun?

Boosting Face Time

One of the first contests at OST was a Face-to-Face Sales Contest. At the time we felt our sales people were too content sitting at their desks and not making enough effort to spend time with their clients in person. So we decided to have a contest that encouraged them to go one-on-one with their customers. In typical OST fashion, we wanted the contest to be unexpected and encourage everyone at the company to be involved.

We developed a simple matrix with the names of our sales, pre-sales, and business development people down the left-hand column and little boxes to the right that could be filled to indicate the number of clients they met with face-to-face. We ran the contest for two months and shared the updated matrix with all OST employees every week. To get the whole company engaged, we allowed them to place bets as if it were a horse race. The employees did not bet actual money, but they could win cash and prizes. The sales team was incentivized by making $10 for every client they met with and an additional $150 for first place, $100 for second place, and $50 for third place, paid out at the end of the two-month contest.

This contest was so effective that we ran it a second time a few years later, and we have had similar contests as well. Part of the magic that makes these contests work is the friendly peer pressure and company-wide involvement. Our culture of trust, fun, and transparency makes such events feel natural. The added benefit is the liveliness and buzz it adds to the office environment. We're to the point now where employees excitedly anticipate discovering what the next wacky contest will be.

If you want a healthy, productive culture in the context of your company, you will find contests and competitions create a bond of belonging even as they recognize individual "winners." You don't have to wait until your culture is mature to introduce contests. If you're having a hard time coming up with an idea about what kind of competition to sponsor, have a company-wide contest to create the next company-wide contest!

So What Does This Mean to You?

Contests energize your people and add an element of fun to your work environment. They can also be used to successfully change behaviors and encourage specific results.

If you are already into contests, maybe one of the contests I described will inspire you to do something similar or maybe they sparked a new creative idea. Most companies introduce contests opportunistically; you may want to consider making contests a priority and scheduling them regularly throughout year.

If contests are relatively new to you, now is the time to get started. Your first contest doesn't have to be anything earth-shattering; just take an idea and go with it. If you are not wildly successful with your first contest, learn from your mistakes and try again.

Shrink-Wrap and Shuffleboards

Adventures in Taking Fun Seriously

CHAPTER THEME SONG:
GOOD TIMES ROLL, THE CARS

You can't take life too seriously and we don't at OST. I once asked a retired friend how he kept his days interesting. He told me that he looks for opportunities to have as much fun as possible, just like we do at OST. For example, the other day he said that he and his wife went into town and browsed one of the local shops. They were only in there for about fifteen minutes, but when they came out, a policeman was writing out a parking ticket.

My friend went up to him and said, "How about giving a senior citizen a break?" The police officer rolled his eyes and continued writing the ticket. So my friend called him a less-than-flattering name. The police officer glared at him and started writing another ticket for having worn tires. So my friend's wife called him her own less-than-flattering name. He finished the second ticket and put it on the windshield with the first. Then he started writing a third ticket. This went on for about twenty minutes. The more they badgered him, the more tickets he wrote. Personally, they didn't care. They came into town by bus.

Joking aside, we do try to pack a lot of fun into OST each day.

A few years ago, one of our employees was away from the office so we thought we'd have some fun. When he walked into his office, he found his desk completely shrink-wrapped and duct-taped. You couldn't see a speck of the desk itself. It took him at least a half hour to unwrap it. You should have seen the look of exasperation on his face. It was one of our proudest accomplishments! Nothing says "we missed you" like a shrink-wrapped desk. With all the rules, regulations, and call for political correctness in our world, it is refreshing when companies buck the system—just a little. And please understand, we don't engage in favoritism or individual harassment here—we would have done the same for any of our people!

Over the past ten years we have gone through five dart boards—three old-fashioned boards with metal darts and a couple of electronic ones. Clearly, they get a lot of use. Let's face it, work and its collateral damage, also known as stress, take an enormous toll. Researchers estimate a typical person's career is comprised of something like 80,000 hours. That's a lot of hours! At OST we decided a long time ago we were going to lighten up as much as possible, not take ourselves too seriously, and take our best shot at enjoying each and every day. We realize that having some fun along the way, like playing darts, is only one small piece of our culture puzzle, but it is an essential one.

Let the Good Times Roll

This may be hard to believe, but I have genuinely loved coming into work every day for the past ten plus years. On those rare occasions when I felt the fun starting to slip away, I found ways to make it fun again. Selfishly, I want every day to be enjoyable and fulfilling, but I also know what a critical role this upbeat environment plays in the health of our company's culture. We continually hear visitors comment on the positive vibe in the air at OST, which is music to our ears (Let the Good Times Roll.)

Often these same visitors ask us if we are trying to emulate companies like Google. The answer is no, and for some reason I don't like it when people compare OST's culture to others. We pride ourselves on being creative and unique. Like siblings striving to distinguish themselves, we like to think we are our own company.

Over the years, our corporate toy box has included a Play-Station 2, a Nintendo Wii, a remote-control glider with water pontoons, two shuffleboard tables, and an iPad-controlled hovercraft. We held a "Bring Your Dog to Work Day," my Yellow Lab, Cali, being the only dog to pee on the carpet. Our chili cook-offs are legendary. We brought in our own barista for a week. Other activities have included secret Santa, minor league baseball summer parties, an overnight trip to a horse ranch with a water park and a rodeo, and a random party on our deck with a live band and buffet. We also host not so occasional afternoon happy hours.

Our people are self-motivated and have an excellent work ethic, so finding a way to add a little recreation into their day is rewarding. Playtime has a way of reviving one's spirits and even increasing productivity.

Making Our Clients Our Friends

When we can we like to include our clients in this good-natured frivolity. Some have policies against such entertainment, and though we don't completely understand that point of view, we certainly abide by their rules. But for those clients who allow it, as often as possible we nudge them into the deep end of our culture pool. We truly believe cultivating personal relationships outside business helps to build trust with our clients and partners. Ultimately it leads to improved productivity for both parties (pun intended).

As you may have guessed, we've devised some creative ways to spend time with our clients in addition to traditional corporate excursions like golf, meals, sporting events, and the like. We have taken customers on overnight fishing trips with guides and a private chef, a day of hunting for pheasant and quail, a quad ATV tour, a couple hours at the shooting range, and weekend getaways.

You might wonder when we have time to, uh, work. We do too. But somehow the projects get done and done well.

Whether you're skeptical or totally on board, I hope there's at least a part of you asking "Hey, does OST have any openings?" We get that a lot, but as the past captain of this ship (or captain wannabe as my friend Gary calls me), I'm the first to admit that having fun isn't enough. It has to be part of other critical variables in work culture, and I do address these in later chapters. Here I just wanted to stress the importance of taking fun seriously as a core dynamic in a healthy corporate culture.

OST Fun Days

A couple years ago we decided to gather the entire OST team with the sole purpose of having fun. We strained our collective genius to come up with a unique name. Thirty seconds later "OST Fun Days" was born. We flew in OST employees from locations around the country, so they could spend two days getting to know each other and, well, having fun. Given the excruciating effort we put into the name, we wanted to keep the rules simple: "We just want to have fun—no speeches, no business, and no cliques."

When the employees arrived at noon on a Thursday, we had the "What the Truck" food truck waiting for them in the parking lot. We had the most-amazing-designer-cupcakes-on-planet-earth for dessert. After lunch and some time to let the cupcakes settle, we all gathered in the OST kitchen (don't let me forget to tell you about our kitchen!). Jim VanderMey, our chief innovation officer, had planned a road rally that would send us racing all over town chasing down clues. I wasn't so sure about this idea when Jim first proposed it. It seemed like it might not appeal to everyone, and honestly, I thought it sounded cheesy. After all, we were spending an enormous amount of money to get everyone together, and we didn't want to take the chance at a flop.

Boy was I wrong. The road rally was a huge success! Teams were made up of five or six people with the intention of encouraging interaction across functional areas and geographical locations, leveling any perceived hierarchies. The road rally included clues with GPS coordinates, a bull's head, a grand piano, and a splash in a downtown fountain. It was überdorky in the best possible, comradery-building way. You could sense the high level of engagement and energy by the bickering over which teams deserved to win at the awards ceremony. Then it was off to Cygnus restaurant, located atop the Amway Grand Plaza Hotel. We reserved the entire restaurant to enjoy a great meal, with great people, overlooking the city we had conquered a few hours earlier.

The next morning employees each picked one of the following activities to enjoy: riding in a hot-air balloon, sailing on Lake Michigan, relaxing at the spa, kayaking on the Grand River, fishing on a Lake Michigan charter boat, or cooking at chef school. The biggest hit was that last one where teams were trained by chefs at the acclaimed JW Marriot and competed to see who could come up with the best creation. Meredith Bronk created an OST appetizer so tasty it showed up on the menu at the JW for a time.

After everyone returned from their half-day events, we gave them some time to relax while they enjoyed wood-fired pizzas and exchanged stories before heading home. The only thing that may have made the event better would have been including spouses, significant others, and families. (That one depended on who you asked.) But everyone agreed OST Fun Days more than lived up to the enormous pressure imposed by the name.

Companies that make their employees their top priority naturally take the time and energy to coordinate events like Fun Days. It is even more important, though, to make fun a part of every workday.

I haven't mentioned all the little things—like lunch brought in by OST once or a twice a week, folks ribbing each other on our internal Facebook page, participating in community events together. Rubber band fights, OST employees forming a band to play rock-and-roll music for us at a kickoff, an employee bringing in twenty pounds of salmon for anyone to take some home, and a couple employees bringing in their smokers to grill lunch for everyone. These are only a few of the things we've done and continue to do.

There's no "right way" to stoke fun in your company's culture. I only hope these examples spark some ideas for ways to lighten up your own offices.

Not Your Typical Work Party

We've all attended work parties that were more obligation than party—the ones that just make you uncomfortable, because of the politics, the boring speeches, the people you don't much like, the pretentiousness, or the general unease of it all. Around here we try hard to throw company parties with a capital P—the kind that families eagerly anticipate because they are a blast for everyone. The OST summer party typically includes employees, spouses, and children. Examples of summer parties we've logged over the years include a day trip to a Lake Michigan beach house with a catered meal, breakfast at a Lake Michigan beach resort, a day at the Michigan Adventure theme park, an employee game at the West Michigan Whitecaps baseball park, and a day at a Silver Lake cottage (dune rides included).

MSU vs. U of M

Like many companies we also have fun with intrastate sports rivalries. Most people in Michigan bleed Spartan green for Michigan State University (MSU) or Wolverine blue for the University of Michigan (U of M), and our employees are no exception.

Three years ago, Dan Frank, an OST sales executive and long-time employee, lost our annual MSU vs. U of M football bet. Michigan State won! That meant Dan was required to "proudly display" a Sparty doll on his desk from October through the end of the year. Dan was a good sport and in full compliance until the day his eleven-year-old daughter, Natalie, and her best friend, Tori, dressed Sparty in a U of M cheerleading outfit. One thing led to another, and before you knew it, a full-blown war had broken out. I wrote a formal complaint to which the girls recorded their audio file response:

Dear Mr. Behm,

We are afraid you are extremely wrong. The Wolverines are a symbol of smartness—obviously, and pure awesomeness. We would like to inform you that the bet was to display the winning team's mascot; it never said that it had to display all of the mascot. Therefore Daniel Frank displayed Sparty in a quite attractive University of Michigan cheerleading outfit. In fact you should thank Daniel Frank and his amazing daughter, me, Natalie, for making Sparty one hundred percent more attractive and less ugly. Obviously with Sparty dressed in his favorite team's outfit he is happier. So we would like to point out that he looks totally re-donk-ulous in his fighting armor that he clearly never uses. We hope you understand that maize is the color of the sun and without it the world would be dark and cold. Blue is the color of everyone's favorite flavor of Jolly Ranchers. We hope that you realize that green is the color of Brussels sprouts and as we both know nobody likes Brussels sprouts.

Your very right, awesome Wolverine friends,
Natalie Frank and Victoria Bronk

Ha ha, hee hee, ho, ho—Go Michigan!

I laughed so hard I played the audio recording for the entire company at the next annual kickoff meeting. And I still regret my failure to edit out the "Go Michigan!" at the end. This is what a fun culture is all about.

Keeping It Real

At this point you may think OST is living in la-la land and that I don't have a clue about the real world. You might even think we've lost touch with reality.

Let me assure you, we're not perfect. There are times when OST is an ugly place. Times when we have handled people situations poorly, times when we have made decisions we are ashamed of, times when we have taken whatever we can get for ourselves, and times when we have been hypocrites. We are definitely human.

But most days, life is pretty good here. There's no place I would rather have my desk shrink-wrapped than OST.

So What Does This Mean to You?

Just for fun, I pulled up a list of the one hundred most famous people of the twentieth century to see if any of them were known specifically for having fun—Marilyn Monroe, Mother Teresa, John F. Kennedy, Martin Luther King, Nelson Mandela, Winston Churchill, Bill Gates, Muhammad Ali, Mahatma Gandhi, Margaret Thatcher . . . Nope. So maybe you won't become famous by focusing on fun, but I do believe that you will improve your employee work experience.

Okay—I'll admit it—we do take fun to an extreme at OST. So I am not going to ask you to start shrink-wrapping your employees' desks, but I will tell you that socializing and having fun with coworkers creates a bond and fosters camaraderie which results in lower turnover and higher job satisfaction. As a matter of fact, research has shown that happy employees perform at a much higher level than those who are not happy.

What is your company's take on having fun in the workplace? If it needs a little boost consider some of the following ideas: employee picnics, community sports leagues, bring-your-dog-to-work day, gift exchanges, community volunteering, a company band, ice cream socials, a chili cook-off, holiday parties, chair massages, costume contests, golf outings, bowling outings, a photo booth, video game day—the possibilities are endless.

Take action to have more fun today!

A Wedding in India

Other Ways to Care for Employees

CHAPTER THEME SONG:
"IF EVERYONE CARED," NICKELBACK

One of the best decisions we ever made as a company was to hire Bhaskar Gunda. Well known in our industry for his unusually broad set of skills, Bhaskar is the kind of guy who can take any technology project—no matter how complex—and make it work. He is also one of the hardest workers I have ever met, not to mention being smart, tenacious, and marvelously good-natured.

When Bhaskar first came to OST, most people had a hard time pronouncing his name. Spelled phonetically it's Bhaskar Goonda, so we all playfully remembered his first name by thinking of a boxcar— boxcar goonda. Bhaskar moved to Grand Rapids with his wife and three girls, but he didn't see them much because he worked around the clock—literally! In fact, he single-handedly generated as much revenue as two "typical" consultants. Eventually it caught up with him, and Bhaskar suffered health problems for a period of years from overexertion. Today he's trying to practice more work-life balance, and I'm happy to report he's healthy and going strong.

Over the years Bhaskar gave up so much of himself for OST that our leadership team—our entire company—wanted to do something special for him in return. Because he had been on the road for many months, away from our main office, we suspected he might be feeling isolated. With a little cultural research, we discovered that people from India often value formal recognition as a sign of great honor. So Jim VanderMey and I decided to travel to India to honor Bhaskar formally for his significant contributions to our company. We jointly signed the following letter with our intentions.

October 2, 2008

Bhaskar,

We are thankful for your numerous contributions and many sacrifices you have made on behalf of OST over the past eight and a half years. As a gesture of our appreciation, we would like to travel to your home in India to present you with a service award for your dedication to OST.

You are welcome to invite friends and family to this celebration and all of the costs for catering a meal and renting a facility will be covered by the company. Just let us know if there is anything we can do to assist with the planning.

We would like the timing of this event to fit with you and your family's schedule; we are flexible, so any time over the next six to nine months is okay with us. Just let us know a couple months in advance so we can make travel arrangements.

We are looking forward to visiting you in India, which is something Jim and I have talked about doing for a long time. You have been—and continue to be—one of the cornerstones of our company and we value your friendship.

Sincerely,

Dan Behm, President

Jim VanderMey, CTO

Bhaskar was overcome with a combination of pride, humility, and joy—exactly what we were hoping for. After some thought he let us know that he would like to time our visit to coincide with the marriage of his oldest daughter, a union that was being arranged back in India. Two years and three astrologists later (they had to agree on the exact date, time, and minute for the ceremony), Jim and I were off to India to honor Bhaskar and to celebrate his daughter's wedding with him and his family.

The weeklong celebration fascinated me, making for an unforgettable trip in which Bhaskar and his family honored us more than we honored him. Bhaskar brought us to the marriage site the day before the wedding to see the progress that two hundred workers hurried to complete: carpenters were constructing facades, florists were decorating with thousands of flowers, and chefs had begun preparations for over fifteen hundred guests.

The spectacular wedding service culminated as the parents of the bride and groom joined the couple's hands under a banner placed between them, so they could not see each other until the appointed time. The parents then lifted the banner at the exact time the astrologists had specified. Talk about a dramatic reveal! I've never seen anything as uniquely beautiful as their ceremony.

Later in the week Jim and I honored Bhaskar with presentations to his friends and family in the top floor of the finest hotel in town. During the ceremony the audience showed their admiration for Bhaskar with flowers and gifts. I have never been snapped in more pictures—including those taken at my *own* wedding. It was a true celebration—along with an impressive spread of delicious Indian food.

Traveling to India was our way of thanking Bhaskar for being a great friend and dedicated employee. He responded by blessing Jim and me through his appreciation and hospitality. Bhaskar was the consummate ambassador of our company culture, caring for us even as we worked to care for him.

Helping Your Employees Help Others

When you are building a company culture based on nurturing your employees and their families, it is important to realize that your employees' lives extend beyond work and home. Every once in a while, we find ways to touch the lives of other people, within our employees' network of relationships, such as our annual March Madness Open House. We encourage employees to invite their friends and extended families so people they care about can experience OST firsthand.

Our Friends and Family Assistance Grants are another example of reaching out to people who are important to our employees. Most people know someone hurting financially, so we give our employees a two-week window to let us know about someone special who could use a little help—a relative, an acquaintance from church or a community group, a close friend, neighbor, or friend of a friend. Our employees know we will consider every request and we'll work to provide at least some level of support for every opportunity. We also emphasize that we're not looking for a PR splash for OST; in fact, we try to keep the gifts as anonymous as possible. We prefer not to give money but instead agree to pay bills or to provide the goods or services needed.

In one instance, out of eighteen requests, we provided significant levels of assistance to all but one of them. We ask our employees to provide as much information as possible so we can determine how best to help. If someone has lost their job and is unable to pay their electric bill, our employee will find out how much is owed and provide us with a contact at the electric company. Keeping the employees involved helps to validate the need and provides them with the opportunity to participate in the giving.

Here's one of the actual requests we were able to fulfill. Situations like this one keep us motivated to work together and make community service more than a buzzword.

Dear Dan and Meredith,

This email comes at a really interesting time for me. I am not sure how much either of you know about Devon and Dante, the two little boys that I have been mentoring over the past three years, but they recently moved to Alaska. Their father, Tyrese, has a sister who lives there, and he felt the need to get away from some bad influences here in Grand Rapids and give his kids a fresh start.

I commend him for doing this, but it's been a huge struggle. Tyrese has been fighting poverty his entire life, and his girlfriend became pregnant with Devon when they were both fourteen and with Dante when they were sixteen. Tyrese has had full custody of the boys since he turned twenty years old. I spend time with these boys every week. Tyrese is an incredibly loving father and does everything he can to be a positive influence on his kids, but— as you can imagine—with limited resources and no safety net, just putting food on the table is a constant grind.

Tyrese recently had his car taken for driving without updated insurance and my request is to help pay the $500 it would cost to get his car back (and help cover the insurance). He was forced to resign from a job that he had just started because he has had no way of getting there.

I am planning to fly out there this summer and use some resources that a local nonprofit has provided in order to help him make a plan—whether that means staying in Alaska or moving his boys back to Michigan (which is my hope).

If you have additional guidance that you'd like to share—I'm all ears. This relationship is one of the most important in my life and I just want to do whatever I can to help. That family has become an extension of my family. They were the first people to spend the night at my house when I moved in, some of my first visitors at OST, and in the middle of the Polar Vortex this winter they never hesitated helping me shovel my sidewalk after I would pick them up from school. They are honestly the nicest kids. Some days, totally out of the blue, they will ask if we can go pack suppers at Kids' Food Bank or make cookies for their granny. Sometimes it just takes having the support you need to get where you're going. I know for sure I wouldn't be anywhere close to where I am today if I didn't have appropriate guidance from a devoted family and community. Thank you for any help you can provide.

Sincerely,
[OST Employee]

This employee used OST funds and contributed some of his own money to get Tyrese's car back. Now Tyrese has a fighting chance.

Letting Someone Go . . . Carefully

It is one thing to help people in need and to be generous and thoughtful with employees who are performing well and fit into the culture, but how do you care for employees in the midst of difficult situations? If the true test of a leader is how he or she carries on when times are tough, the same is true when it comes to managing employees. It's easy to guide overachieving employees who love their jobs, but what do you do with team members who don't fit, aren't pulling their weight, or simply don't work out?

We've had a few of these situations, and I recall a few years ago how we handled one of these employees who wasn't working out so well. He was friendly, tried his best, cared about others, and was a team player. The problem wasn't his intentions or character, but his capabilities. In many ways this is one the most difficult employee situations to address. A belligerent employee with a bad attitude is easier to confront head-on—you don't feel so bad doing it.

Over time we realized this employee was incapable of doing his job at an acceptable level. He was having difficulty connecting even the simplest of dots and repeatedly made mistakes that negatively affected clients. It was also becoming unfair to his coworkers because they had to cover up and sometimes assist in the cleanup.

We did everything we could to make it work. We thought about other jobs within OST that might be a better fit, and although we tried to focus on his capabilities, it still wasn't working out. Eventually he made a big mistake that required us to fire him. While it was tempting to blame him for his termination and make the company look better, we tried to take the high road. We let him know his mistake had cost him the job, but we did not announce it within the building. We gave him time to look for another position, and when he found one, we threw a going away party for him. We announced that he had found a great position at another company, and we were supporting him and wishing him well.

Disingenuous? Maybe. Enabling? Possibly. But I'm not so sure. Caring for employees means caring for all of them, not the model employees. Everyone deserves to be treated with dignity, unless they won't let you treat them that way. The actions we took with this employee have everything to do with our culture of focusing on our people and their families first. We truly did wish him well!

If you desire a company culture that cares for its employees, it must be a top priority and part of every decision you make. After a while it becomes engrained in your company DNA and will effortlessly figure in without your even thinking about it.

So What Does This Mean to You?

There are so many things an employer can do to care for its employees and this chapter provides just a few examples.

If you really want to do something special for someone, put yourself in their shoes and think about what is most important to them, like we did for Bhaskar. Too often, when trying to do something nice for someone, we think about what we would like instead of what they would like. For example, if an employee continually talks about movies and you know they don't have the extra cash, giving them a gift certificate from their favorite movie theater will mean much more to them than cash. Think about something special that you can do for your top-performing employees today; at minimum, consider handwritten notes to thank them for everything they do for the company.

Find ways to engage your employees with the community—this is a great team-building exercise and brings value to the community at the same time. Employees take pride in their community work which contributes positively to the company culture. Consider giving your employees paid time off every year for community service.

Always treat your employees right, but if you must let someone go, make sure to keep the person's best interest in mind. There is nothing to be gained by broadcasting negative comments.

Make Yourself Comfortable

The Culture-Shaping Power of Your Physical Space

CHAPTER THEME SONG:
"A DAY IN THE LIFE," THE BEATLES

Have you ever heard this quote from Winston Churchill? "We shape our buildings and afterwards our buildings shape us." Most people underestimate the impact physical environment has on a company's culture. We certainly did back when we first started OST.

Like many companies, OST began in a humble office environment with cheap furniture and even cheaper used cubicles. Our building was in a suburban industrial area near light manufacturing plants. Awkwardly wedged among warehouses and distributors, the place looked pleasant enough on the outside but felt cramped and a bit uninspiring on the inside. We spent seven years at this location and it served us adequately, but it was not a place anyone wanted to show off.

We tried to make the most of it. We set up a grill on the deck that was used occasionally for cookouts at lunchtime and occasionally for small meetings. The deck overlooked a man-made, boomerang-shaped pond. We launched our first toys there—two remote control boats that were promised to our employees for achieving performance goals. The pond was also where one of our employees affectionately deposited two goldfish that he named "Dan" and "Jim"—which we never saw again after their initial entry.

The grassy area framing our small pond became a playground. While the pond was muddy and certainly not swimmable, we found other creative uses for our office's backyard. One of our favorites was lunchtime golf: we designated target areas across the pond, and the person to chip closest to the target won the hole. Our lunch hour provided enough time for nine holes of golf . . . with a few minutes left over to eat.

I remember one warm summer day when I was playing golf at the pond with one of our employees. We laughed about our light-hearted competition, especially when one of us would duff one into the water. Late in the game we were chipping across the longest portion of the pond—still only a pitching wedge distance—when my friend topped one and sent the ball sailing into the lot next door. It all happened so quickly, first the sound of the ball hitting the side of a car followed by my friend's expletive. We sheepishly wandered over to the parking lot, relieved to find no witnesses of the event. We found the car and left a note on the windshield along with a brief account of what had happened and our phone number. Surprisingly, the owner of the car never contacted us, but it would be weeks before we were playing golf around the pond again.

Having fun at work is risky at times.

We launched other traditions in this humble little office as well. We started semiobsessively watching the first two days of the NCAA March Madness basketball tournament together. We had a color television set with a built-in VCR and a ten-inch screen, ostensibly used for self-study training courses. Without cable in the building we used the built-in "rabbit ear" antennas with foil wrapped around them for better reception. Whenever the reception faltered, we just moved the ears or rattled the foil so that we could see what was going on. The television was placed in our small conference room—along with the love seat from the reception area—providing a comfortable place to watch the basketball games whenever we could break away.

New Digs

But after seven years we had outgrown our office and started looking for a new one. We needed more space—that was obvious—but also hoped for an environment that better conveyed the image of a high-end professional IT services company. A bit like taking a hot date to a bingo game, we felt a little embarrassed bringing clients—whom we charged $190 an hour—to our current office. After reviewing our options and budget, we chose a classic loft-style office in an old brick manufacturing building on the edge of downtown. Repurposed with tall ceilings and substantial beams, it was a great space, both classic and contemporary.

We anticipated a favorable response to our new office, but what we experienced was off the charts. During the first month the number of positive comments amazed us. It wasn't long before we realized that we had seriously underestimated the value of work environment. There was nothing wrong with our original office, but the new space seemed to generate a positive fun vibe which energized us all. Not only that, our friends, family, clients, and prospective clients now became regular visitors. They liked coming by—whether for a scheduled meeting or just a cup of coffee. Employees were also putting in more hours, which led to increased productivity.

We learned firsthand that the appearance of an office heavily influences how employees and clients feel about the company. This may not seem logical, but emotional responses aren't necessarily logical. People are visual beings, and an attractive physical office has had a substantially positive impact on our business. It may be tough to put a dollar amount on that impact, but I have no doubt it has been significant. Our culture of fun and creativity has increased just as dramatically. The two seem to go hand in hand. I'll say it again: happy employees are productive employees.

From Rubble to Amazing

We stayed in our second office for five years and added square footage twice. Then we reached a point again where we needed more space. During that time there was a significant tax break being offered for offices on the other side of the river, which was very attractive to us. I found an old three-story warehouse—the former Drueke board game factory.

A developer had already refaced the outside of the building, but the inside wasn't much more than an empty shell. I'll never forget taking my colleague and friend (now president) Meredith Bronk to the building for the first time and seeing her reaction as her heels sunk into the dirt floor on the first level. Eyeing the rickety staircase, she asked, "Are you sure it's safe?" Describing my vision for the interior renovation, I was trying to convince her how beautiful it would be given the brickwork, large beams, and tall ceilings. In her ever-gracious way Meredith responded, "You know I trust you."

The construction project lasted six months. We wanted the building designed specifically for us: both the culture we had already formed and the culture we hoped to be. We wanted a building that would encourage visitors to feel welcome and provide an efficient, relaxed environment for our employees. We brainstormed ways to make the space special and ended up designing a 1,500 square foot kitchen with granite countertops, and gorgeous custom cabinets made of white oak along with a fireplace in the reception area, to help people feel at home. It always sets people back when they first walk into our office; "A kitchen? This is beautiful; I love this space!" is a typical comment.

Providing an office space that's attractive and attuned to productivity lets employees, visitors, and clients know that we are proud of our work, our surroundings, and our people. We incorporated quiet areas, common spaces, kitchens, and conference rooms named after board games like backgammon, checkers, chess, and cribbage that were manufactured there, in the old Drueke days.

People at OST take pride in making every visitor feel welcome.

The OST Kitchen

It doesn't matter who they are—a delivery person, family member, customer, friend, the cleaning staff, business partners, or someone simply looking for directions. We want everyone to feel a positive interaction with our company. If we're successful, each return visit through OST's doors should say, "This is a good place to be."

Offering fun alternatives for taking breaks, such as darts, shuffleboard, and Nintendo Wii, along with a fully stocked gym, allows people to have a little fun, relieve some stress, and foster friendships with coworkers.

Supplying drinks and snacks for employees and visitors, or bringing in a meal for everyone, extends the family atmosphere, which is so fundamental to the OST way. From a shared cup of coffee to a catered Mexican lunch, we are brought together in a way that unites us beyond our work.

Our annual March Madness viewing on the old ten-inch TV with foil-covered rabbit ears has evolved into an Open House featuring a dozen flat-screen TVs displaying multiple games simultaneously. We now host almost a thousand guests each year during this eight-hour community extravaganza. We spoil anyone and everyone with nonstop meals, snacks, and desserts from noon until well into the evening. Since this is our signature event, we go all out offering valet parking, gifts, and a thousand dollars in March Madness Basketball Pool cash prizes. It's a blast and we all look forward to this event every year.

The Value of Space

Many out-of-town clients have never seen our work environment in person. One such client had been doing business with us for ten years. A Fortune 500 company, its leaders were considering OST for a large project—even by their standards. So three of their top IT executives decided they'd better cover their bases and travel to our office, to make sure we could handle the work. We had tried to talk them into coming for years and were thrilled with their decision to visit.

We knew from experience our odds of success were extremely high if we spent the necessary time preparing our message and an equally good job communicating it. The day arrived, and we were pumped. We gave them a tour of the building, had a productive meeting, and then hosted a casual lunch in our kitchen area.

We enjoyed meeting with them and hoped they felt the same way. This was later confirmed when the client contacted our account executive and praised OST's preparation for the meetings. He went on to say that we really made them feel welcome and they loved our work environment. He asked, in a kidding sort of way, if we had any job openings. These were the best praises they could give us!

You may be thinking, "Sure, I'd love a building with a 1,500 square foot kitchen, but we can only afford 500 square feet for the whole office!" I completely understand. We started humbly and grew into a larger office space when we could afford to be more deliberate about the kind of work atmosphere we wanted. Now, when we open offices in new locations, we start with cost-effective spaces until profits warrant the expense of a more upscale office. But even with these "starter offices" we do our best to make them feel fun—while still being professional, warm, and homey—to attract the kind of people we want to work with, employees and clients.

Sometimes it feels like we're known more for our buildings than we are for our technology services, but that's okay too. If a picture is worth a thousand words, the place where you work must be worth that many more. Workspace may be only one of many pieces of your company's image puzzle, but don't underestimate the impact it can have on your culture and ultimately your profitability.

So What Does This Mean to You?

How do your employees, clients, friends, and partners feel when they walk into your office space? Does it represent the culture and image that you are hoping to portray? If it does, I am guessing that you are well on your way to success. If not, consider making changes that fall within your means. Even an inexpensive facelift to an undesirable building can make a world of difference. If you are already successful as a business and are thinking that you didn't need a great space to get there why should you improve your space now? I say—improve your space—you will be pleasantly surprised with the business-related results!

PART THREE

HOW WE DO THINGS

Operations, Recruitment, and Partnerships

Fresh Air and Transparent Annual Kickoffs

Frequent Communication in an Age of Secrets and Subterfuge

CHAPTER THEME SONG:
"867-5309/JENNY," TOMMY TUTONE

Dick Cheney and George W. Bush were having breakfast at the White House. The attractive young waitress asked Cheney what he would like, and he replied, "I'd like a bowl of oatmeal and some fruit."

"And what can I get for you, Mr. President?"

George W. looked up from his menu and replied with his trademark wink and slight grin, "How about a quickie this morning?"

"Why, Mr. President!" the waitress exclaimed. "How rude! You're starting to act like President Clinton," and then she stormed away.

Cheney leaned over to Bush and whispered, "It's pronounced 'keesh.'"

How to Communicate During a Recession

You've heard the real estate expression "location, location, location." In business, the secret to success is communication, communication,

communication. This, as anyone who has ever sat in a meeting or had a conversation with their team leaders knows, is easier said than done. To promote a healthy culture in the workplace, communication must include honesty, consistency, and responsiveness—a clear commitment to the ongoing process of understanding one another.

Like many business leaders, I've learned to appreciate the value of communication the most in the midst of a crisis. In October 2008 the great recession barreled through, leveling everything in its wake. Like most businesses, OST had not anticipated the sudden economic downturn, and it didn't take long for us to realize we were in for a world of hurt. A month earlier we had projected strong fourth-quarter revenue and net profit results. What we got was the worst quarter in years with an overall loss in net profit. We hoped the faucet would gradually slow to a trickle, but it had run dry in an instant.

The press was having a field day. Drawing on present conditions as their ammunition, they predicted doom and gloom for decades to come. Beginning in 2008 and throughout 2009, each headline toppled the next, dominos of bad news: "Bubble Burst," "Black Monday," "Lining Up for a Job Fair," "Debt Looms," "Brutal Year," "Economy Falters," "Cutback," "Recession—Tight Credit," "Thousands Lose Homes," and on and on. It was a depressing time for workers in every sector, and our workplace was not exempt. Everyone was concerned about their job, retreating "into their shells" and bracing for the next inevitable blow.

Our leadership team at OST was just as scared as everyone else, so we met and formulated a plan. The first thing we did was decide how much money we could afford to lose before we would have to carry out a more drastic plan, such as laying off employees. The second thing we did was communicate exactly what we were thinking with our employees, making it clear that if we did not go below a certain level of loss, they were secure in their jobs. We emphasized that our objective was to get through the recession without laying off a single employee, and so we started sending out a revenue and net profit email every month, allowing our employees to see exactly where we stood at all times. Our employees really appreciated this. It gave them comfort in knowing that if we maintained a certain level they had nothing to worry about.

A Lot of Fresh Air

By the end of 2008 I was so sick of the negative headlines and news bombarding us every day, I decided to do something about it. Despite the recession, we had plenty of positive things happening at our company, so I committed to send an email newsletter with an encouraging message to our employees once a week starting in January 2009. I called the newsletter "Fresh Air," and the early issues all ended with the statement "We have decided not to participate in the recession."

In addition to the monthly revenue and profit update as well as the "Fresh Air" emails, we used several other methods to keep communication flowing. We regularly conducted employee surveys and made the results available for everyone to see. They consistently reflected our employees' high morale even during a crippling economy. Our company's positivity, in turn, contributed to our solid financial outcomes. As a result, we did not lay off any employees and came out of the recession stronger than ever. Our employees were thankful we continued to hold them and their families as our top priority, especially during the worst of times. They were equally grateful we frequently communicated what was going on in the company with an honest, responsive message.

At the end of 2009 I checked in with the employees to see if it was okay to drop the weekly "Fresh Air." The answer was a resounding no! Six years later I was still rolling them out and they continue today. Throughout the year I inevitably get a little behind. Fifty-two newsletters are a lot of "Fresh Air"! So as the holidays approach, I often scramble to get the last six to ten completed, and everyone playfully ribs me as I race to complete the last few.

Below are two examples of our "Fresh Air" weekly newsletter.

I include them to give you a better idea of what they are all about in case you want to try something similar for your team. They are brief—always a page or less—and purposefully written in simple language for a quick read. As you can see, there's nothing all that special about them, but we have found that simple, consistent, positive messages of encouragement are powerful.

This "Fresh Air" was written during the first month after Meredith Bronk was promoted to president of OST:

Meredith's Fabulous 15 Minutes with HP CEO Meg Whitman Puts OST Healthcare in the Forefront of HP's Vision

Meredith Bronk, John Thayer, Jim VanderMey and Lori Grinwis are all working the HP global partner conference in Las Vegas, Nevada, this week. On a whim, prior to the trip, OST requested a meeting between OST's newly appointed President Meredith Bronk and HP's President and CEO Meg Whitman; we were all astonished when Meg said yes! You see, Meg Whitman, who runs the largest technology company in the world, is undeniably one of the most powerful women in business today.

In Meredith's words, "When I met with her, where I was admittedly a little bit intimidated, she immediately made me feel at home. We were just sitting and chatting. She clearly wants to make sure we are getting what we need from HP. She is a hands-on leader who asked great questions." Meredith went into the meeting prepared to make an impression and to leverage her time with Meg to advance OST.

Meredith explained OST's unique methodology around our persona workshop and our focus on healthcare. Meg admitted that she could get a meeting with any hospital CIO in the country; so Meredith took her up on it.

By the end of the fifteen-minute session, Meg committed to two action items: (1) looking into creating a technology council specifically for regional or superregional resellers like OST, which, of course, Meredith offered to champion and (2) agreeing to personally call on five hospitals to request meetings. WOW!!

So we are starting with our top five list, a group Meg Whitman will have already contacted. If that works, she will call the next group of five accounts. Meredith was pumped as she exclaimed, "How fun is it that . . . Meg Whitman is going to make cold calls on our behalf? Woo-hoo!"

We love this stuff!

Another illustrative "Fresh Air" provides an update on our London office, which opened in December 2013:

OST London Update

Just before the New Year, OST's Joel Vanderveen arrived at the Docklands Technical Centre (DTC) to occupy the latest opening in OST's Just in Time Data Center (JITDC) program. Since then, OST has been building relationships, presence, and servers outside London's Canary Wharf with our clients. So far, we've sold, configured, and sent out well over 400 servers to three different locations in England and Ireland. To fill the few gaps in time spent in the OST "cave," Joel joined the ranks of one of our client's Ops crew—installing new hardware, cabling new cabinets, and being the butt end of cheeky American jokes. Despite the constant debate over the true definition of "chips," the team in London has done a fantastic job of welcoming Joel into their data center and helped him navigate the near-overwhelming task of moving to London.

However, much of the hard work comes from 4,000 miles west of London: Minneapolis. The Minneapolis team has done a "brilliant" job of coordinating shipping, inventory, and sales over three locations in two countries. Nicole Rademaker, Dave Streitman, Mike Brendon, Brian Dehn, Matt Pince, and our latest additions, Laura Stromberg and Matt Vaziripour, have been doing really great work to ensure every "kit" goes out the door on time and is configured correctly at every location. Additionally, a huge shout-out goes to OST sales and operations for easing the program through the jarring transition from dollars to pounds.

All told, it's safe to say both our clients and Joel are "chuffed to bits" (very pleased) with the start of the program in London. The feedback we've received from our clients has been positive; and with a growing emphasis on this data center location, we are confident there will continue to be at least one OSTer adding milk and sugar to his Earl Grey tea.

We love this stuff!!

The Annual Kickoff

Even during the best of times, we do everything possible to communicate continually about our vision for the future, our financial and organizational results, and our desires and expectations. In addition to "Fresh Air" newsletters, we continue to report our financial results to our employees every month. This is somewhat unusual for a privately held company, but our employees truly appreciate the openness.

Other methods of regular employee communication include a detailed company update report two times a year (this is an eight- to ten-page document describing the state of the company), a company-wide conference call every other month, a monthly newsletter called "The Hardwire," our blog called the *OST Kitchen*, a weekly detailed billable hours report, a one-page company dashboard updated quarterly, and an annual kickoff meeting that everyone attends.

This annual kickoff meeting is where we set the tone for the year. We invest an enormous amount of preparation into the meeting, as it is the only day of the year where all our employees are in one room. It's typical that we share the previous year's results, goals for the upcoming year, and our vision for the future, but over the years we have included client and employee panels, outside speakers, rock bands made up entirely of OST employees, and many other creative twists and turns to make it an engaging, energizing day.

Perhaps what makes our kickoff meeting most unique is that it is not just a big pep rally. We also talk about our mistakes and the areas in which we are struggling. This dedication to honesty and corporate self-disclosure is an important part of our culture.

John Vancil, our director of professional services, demonstrated this kind of transparency in our 2015 fiscal year kickoff meeting. John comes from a decidedly "black and white" military background and was brought onboard to improve our company processes. While doing an outstanding job, John knew his shortcomings and wanted to improve himself. After getting 360-degree feedback from his peers, John had a strong desire to start seeing those shades of grey transformed into full color.

Each of the directors on our leadership team discussed their personal lives to help employees relate to them as everyday people. Following suit, John described his wishes to improve himself and shared the details of the 360-degree feedback, including the areas where he needed most work. John, a big, no-nonsense kind of guy, revealed his huge heart that day, even describing himself as a "teddy bear with claws." For those of us who had known John for years, his admissions were pretty incredible. His presentation was rated by the audience as the best speech of the day among many excellent presentations.

A Final Admonition

A relentless dedication to communication remains one of the most important ingredients to business success and healthy cultures. But it must be the real deal. The kind of communication that John Vancil used in his teddy bear with claws speech makes a difference. Communication that is intended only to impress or is perceived as manipulative is useless. Listening to each other and relating authentically to one another remains crucial.

If you want a healthy business culture, tell the truth, keep the communication frequent, and address the issues your employees want and need to understand. If you don't have regular intervals for open communication with your employees, now is the time to start.

So What Does This Mean to You?

If you are like most of us, you will spend thirty-five to forty-five years of your life in the workplace. And if history repeats itself, you will likely experience between six and eight recessions of varying degrees of intensity. How will you react when the next recession comes? How will you communicate with your employees? It is times like these that bring out the best and worst in leaders. Consider letting your employees know how you really feel, what is expected of them, what you are doing to protect their jobs, and what your criteria are for taking drastic action. Do whatever you can to reduce their stress and worry.

Take a moment now to consider a regular "Fresh Air" communication at your company. It is the simplest most effective communication we have at OST.

Think about the regular communication that you have with your employees today and probe for gaps. Consider some of the communications ideas in this chapter and decide if one of them might be right for your company. The bottom line—communicate, communicate, communicate.

············ (13) ············

Talking Frogs
and "One-Percenters"

The Subtle Art of Hiring and Retention

CHAPTER THEME SONG:
"ANOTHER BRICK IN THE WALL," PINK FLOYD

A guy is seventy-two years old and loves to fish.

He is sitting in his boat one day when he hears a voice say "Pick me up." He looks around and can't see anyone. He thinks maybe he's dreaming when he hears the voice again: "Pick me up." He looks in the water and there, floating on the top, is a frog.

"Are you talking to me?" the man asks. "Yes, I'm talking to you," the frog replies. "Pick me up, then kiss me and I'll turn into the most beautiful woman you have ever seen. I'll make sure all your friends are envious because I will be your bride!"

The man looks at the frog briefly, picks it up carefully, and places it in his front pocket. "What, are you nuts?!" the frog exclaims. "Didn't you hear what I said? Kiss me, and I'll be your beautiful bride."

The man opens his pocket, looks at the frog, and says, "Nah, at my age, I'd rather have a talking frog."

Talking Frogs Are Hard to Find

When it comes to hiring the right people, you need an enormous amount of wisdom. Many times, it boils down to this: do you go with the "beautiful bride" or the "talking frog"? Or as Forrest Gump might put it, employees "are like a box of chocolates"—they may look like superstars on paper, but "you never know what you're going to get."

Almost every business book ever written stresses the importance of hiring the right people—and the few that don't should. Since everything revolves around our employees and their families at OST, recruiting and selecting employees who fit into our culture remains vital to our long-term success. So as you might expect, we invest an inordinate amount of thought, time, and effort into finding the perfect match. Talking frogs are hard to find.

Searching for One-Percenters

After my ten-year career at IBM and before starting OST I founded a start-up company called SkyTech International that provided Internet services via satellite. I didn't have a clue what I was doing, and the company failed miserably. During that year I remember meeting with a potential partner that was focusing on the World Wide Web. I will never forget the impressive PowerPoint presentation they gave describing the "information highway."

I was exposed to a lot of bright people during my time at IBM, but I had never been around people as brilliant as these. Their presentation was a step above, using graphics and animation that I had never seen before. The presenters had a flair that wowed me and underscored their vastly superior knowledge on the subject.

The problem was they never let me or anyone else within a ten-mile radius forget how smart they were. The weight of their arrogance became suffocating. Yes, the presentation was great, but I couldn't stand to be around these people and never went back.

This particular incident had a profound impact on hiring practices at OST. We did, in fact, recruit brilliant technologists so that we could provide superior value to our clients. But we refused to tolerate attitude, making every effort only to hire people we felt were humble and genuine. We coined a phrase long before others started using it: "one-percenters." We would look for the absolute best people we could find in the industry with that unique combination of being übersmart and firmly grounded. We called them one-percenters. They were like finding a needle in a haystack (or a talking frog), but we have managed to hire many of them over the years. We don't use the term one-percenter much anymore. These days we tend to describe them as "OST all day long"—as in, "Let's hire her, she's OST all day long."

Our Competitive Advantage

Every successful company can point to their top strengths, which give them a competitive advantage in the marketplace. But without the right people, any company environment eventually stagnates and deteriorates. While I was aware of OST's many strengths, early on we discovered our number one competitive advantage was our ability to recruit and retain the best people. The day I recognized this I was so excited, I tracked down each member of the leadership team to tell them my revelation.

They were not nearly as ecstatic as I was, but they did agree that, given an adequate amount of time, we could hire almost anyone we wanted. So we made the decision to target some of the best people in the industry over a period of years. In most cases we were successful bringing them on board. These were the kind of hires that caused our competitors and clients to marvel: "Wow—can you believe that OST won them over?" We did this again and again and continue to do it today. So how can OST boast this level of hiring success when many companies say hiring good people is their number one struggle? Judging from the feedback of our recruits, I would say it's the result of our culture, though the exact recipe is hard to nail down. In the end, I truly believe it comes down to a sincere commitment to placing our people and their families first.

How We Interview and Hire

Unlike other decisions at OST, which tend to happen pretty quickly, our hiring process at OST can be long and a bit tedious. I'm sure prospective employees have wondered why it takes so long to complete the hiring process after they've been interviewed. Here's the deal: as a company, the most painful experiences are not related to profits, losing deals, or personal conflicts. Nothing is even close to the pain of having to let someone go. We need to be absolutely certain—for their sake and ours—that every person hired is a great fit before we offer them the job.

Please notice the distinction. We're not looking for perfect people, just people "perfect for OST." This is less about job profiles and more about individual people. First and foremost, we want a cultural fit, someone who feels like they're coming home. Desired characteristics in new hires include integrity, humility, positive attitude, tenacity, adaptability, and cooperation. The best way to determine a good match is through several interviews with multiple OST people. These interviews reveal any flaws in the fit (not necessarily in the person), and at the same time we're able to reveal our company to the prospective employee.

Prior to the interviews, each OST interviewer is briefed on their specific role in the interview process and given information on the candidate along with the position for which they are being considered. For example, an interviewer may be asked to probe into the reasons why the candidate had fifteen jobs in the past two years or may be asked to take on the role of selling the candidate on OST (maybe not to the candidate with fifteen jobs!). We hire people for the long term, so we can't afford to make a mistake that could have been prevented by a little due diligence.

In some cases, when someone is either currently unemployed or working as a contractor, we have the flexibility to hire him or her on a conditional basis. We prefer this method to a conventional hire because we can get to know one another over two or three months and discover whether there's a mutual fit. The potential employee evaluates OST to see if this is where she wants to work, and OST evaluates the prospective employee to determine if she has a cultural and skill set match. If not, we can part amicably at the end of the contract period without the challenges of terminating a full-time employee.

Getting the Best People

We spend many planning hours each year determining our strategic direction as a company, including the human resources we'll need to meet our goals. The positions we need to fill are anticipated and actively recruited for, but occasionally we are approached by a phenomenally successful person interested in working for OST in a position we didn't even realize we needed. Until then.

Let's say a technical person recognized as a top talent approaches OST with a strong desire to join us. We may not be looking for a person with their skill set, but let's say this person can introduce us to a new technology we're interested in pursuing. In addition, the confidence, capability, and contacts this person brings might be hard to pass up. We know an opportunity when we see it, and some of our best people have been opportunistic hires.

Everyone knows it makes sense to hire the best people. But too often companies rush their hiring process because of some urgent need within the business. This may extinguish the immediate fire, but it's no way to build a business. The secret to building a culture that will attract the best people is to hire the best people to begin with. People want to work with people they like, people from whom they can learn, and people they respect. The secret to a successful culture is that simple—and that hard.

Mistakes along the Way

We are not immune to blunders at OST. Sometimes we make more than our fair share. Have you ever had the perfect idea you knew couldn't fail? I have them on a regular basis! This optimism sometimes gets the best of me, and I forget there's no such thing as "infallible" in business. One day it occurred to me, for example, "If we are so good at hiring anyone we go after, why not take this to a new level and hire five of the top twenty sales people in our industry in the Midwest?" No-brainer, right?

This would be a game changer for our company as these top people typically sell $10 to $20 million in products and services per year compared to the industry average of $3 to $5 million. I remember telling our team not to be concerned about the cultural fit; after all, sales people of this caliber had to possess high integrity and be great at relationships in order to reach their level of current success.

In a pool of thousands, five of the top twenty sales professionals presented a tall order, but we were up for the challenge. Many of these pros were untouchable because of ironclad noncompetes, but we identified several others as viable targets. In true OST fashion we succeeded in hiring three or four sales people considered top performers in the Midwest. We were proud to accomplish this initiative, and I confess I felt a bit smug about our accomplishment.

I'm sad to say none of these sales reps are still with OST today—even though they were great people. So what went wrong? You guessed it: they didn't fit into our culture. We didn't like the way they interacted with our clients and our employees, and they did not like the way we did business. We tried to help them to fit in, and they also made efforts to fit in, but it just didn't work.

One of these sales reps became furious when we fired her. She couldn't understand why we would fire a person whose sales numbers had *exceeded* expectations. Our leadership team had a terrible feeling in the pit of our collective stomach for days afterward. This is why we typically spend so much time vetting employee candidates—

to avoid situations like this. We knew we were hurting this person and her family. It's the most painful experience we can have as a company, and the worst part is that it could have been prevented.

The Best Compliment

We have not found a foolproof method for hiring, but we are pleased with our overall results. A couple of years ago I was conducting an exit interview with one of our sales people. I hated to see him go, as he was OST all day long—talented, well-liked, bright, and trustworthy. He had only been with OST a year, and I asked him why he was leaving. He said that during the interview process a year ago we had told him that OST was relatively unstructured and entrepreneurial by nature. This appealed to him at the time, but he found he was the kind of person who needed structure.

I asked him what he would change about OST. He said he loved everything about the company and wouldn't change a thing. I pressed him on this point and he held his ground. He then went on to say, "I have worked for some great companies and all of them have had really good people, but there were always a few jerks. The strange thing about OST is that everyone is nice and willing to help—there are no jerks! How do you do that?" It turns out this employee and OST were not a good fit, that just happens sometimes, but he could not have given OST better praise.

So What Does This Mean to You?

Words of wisdom: Hire the best people. Don't settle. Take your time during the hiring process. Assure a cultural fit. Don't assume that a person's success at another company with transfer to your company. Don't be afraid to hire opportunistically if the right person comes along. Avoid people that exhibit arrogance during the interview process. And remember to hire the best people!

Believing in Your Success

Relentless Determination That Surprises People

CHAPTER THEME SONG:
"DON'T STOP BELIEVING," JOURNEY

When I was a new salesman at IBM, I was just naïve enough to question the way things had always been done. Assigned the Herman Miller account (second largest office designer/manufacturer in the world), I was clearly out of my league. One meeting with Herman Miller's director of IT, Johnny Schrotenboer, and it was evident to him too. I didn't find this out until later, but Johnny asked Walt Trock, my manager, to have me taken off the account. He made it clear it was nothing personal, he just preferred an IBM representative with more experience.

Walt Trock was a big man with a powerful personality. I once saw him give a motivational speech that would have qualified as a first-rate TED Talk. Walt was also a master strategist—the best I have ever witnessed—so he convinced Johnny to give me a month or two. If he was still dissatisfied, Walt would then replace me with a more experienced rep.

As a part of the account transition, I met with the IBM rep assigned to the account for the past few years. He told me about a multimillion-dollar purchase that was on the horizon for Herman

Miller—a large mainframe computer. Unfortunately, Herman Miller was planning to acquire it on the used market, so I would not get any credit for the sale. He said it would be a waste of time to convince Herman Miller to purchase a new system, as they were saving over $500,000 by purchasing used.

I love a competitive challenge and wasn't about to miss an opportunity like this one, even if their minds were already made up. So I started to dig into the situation with Don Kines, the IBM Systems Engineer assigned to Herman Miller. He took me through the technical aspects of the deal and explained the details related to the $500,000 savings for the used unit.

My expertise, if you could call it that, was in midrange computers; I knew very little about mainframes.

So I spent a week or two learning more about our current product line and comparing it with Herman Miller's requirements. I learned IBM had just released an air-cooled version of the mainframe, which curiously no one seemed to be discussing for this client's needs.

When I compared Herman Miller's requirements with the new air-cooled mainframe's capabilities, they seemed to match up, with plenty of room for growth. I went to Don with this information, and he quickly shot it down. "Herman Miller is a water-cooled shop, there's no way they would consider an air-cooled mainframe." This seemed strange to me, so I checked with other IBM engineers and reps, and they all agreed with Don and recommended that I not waste my time pursuing it further.

I wasn't ready to let it go.

I contacted Johnny at Herman Miller to request a date to present IBM's recommendation for his upcoming purchase. He cordially agreed to give me one hour with him and his staff but said it would likely be a waste of time because they intended to purchase the used machine. We set a presentation date about a month out, so I would have time to prepare.

The next task was to convince Don that the air-cooled mainframe was the best solution for Herman Miller. My argument was simple: the air-cooled system would cost less overall when you included the electricity dollars to run it and was technically equivalent to the water-cooled mainframe. The only thing we'd have to overcome was perception.

It was not easy, but eventually Don came around. He and I spent the next month building our airtight case (pun intended) and awaited the meeting. This would be my first presentation to Herman Miller, so we worked hard to address every objection, no matter how obscure. Despite my nerves, I was absolutely convinced this was the right solution for our high-profile client's needs.

The big day came. On the way to the conference room, Don and I walked by Johnny's office and noticed a diagram on his whiteboard depicting the used mainframe solution. We knew we had a lot of convincing to do.

The conference room was filled to capacity. I spoke for the first forty-five minutes, then Don finished off the hour. Our presentation seemed to go well, but there were very few questions.

Following the presentation, Johnny walked Don and me down to his office. He went directly to his whiteboard, erased the used mainframe solution and replaced it with the new IBM air-cooled mainframe. Herman Miller placed the order a few weeks later. After a few months, when the new mainframe arrived, Johnny asked me to come in on a Saturday and plug the new computer into power. Johnny also invited us to Herman Miller's executive retreat center for a luncheon to celebrate the installation. I've never felt more honored—before or since.

Tenacity Is a Key Ingredient

On my first three performance reviews at IBM, each of my managers listed tenacity as my best asset. I laugh now because, at the time, it was probably my *only* asset. I didn't know much. After some years in the business I learned to search out tenacious employees to hire. If you look closely enough into their eyes, you can see whether they possess the unyielding resolve of a great employee.

The first thing that comes to mind when I think about our company culture is putting our employees and their families first. The first thing that comes to mind when I think about succeeding at a particular task or new business initiative is tenacity—what I call relentless determination. This is true for our technical people, sales people, leadership team, operations team . . . and just about everyone else. It starts at the ground level with the belief that we can do anything that we set our attention to.

This mindset is one of the primary reasons for OST's success and will continue to drive its success for many years to come. We believe in our people, we believe in each other, we believe in our capabilities, we believe in our company, and deep down we believe that that there isn't anything we can't do. It's woven into the fabric of our culture.

You Need More Than Skill and Polish

When we first opened our Minneapolis office, we hired two of the best people I've ever worked with. These two, one in sales and the other a senior tech, were exceptionally smart, well-known, well-liked, and had deep connections with many of the largest corporations in town. They came from a Fortune 100 company where both were superstars and enjoyed working together. Most importantly they were a perfect cultural fit!

It was a major coup to hire this level of talent, and it felt like this would put us on a fast track to success in Minneapolis. We could hardly believe our good fortune—and neither could our competitors or industry insiders.

Our Minnesota dream-duo quickly learned the OST value proposition and proceeded to call on every account they knew in town, and then some. Their intensity and work ethic impressed everyone in our company. Whenever I visited our Minneapolis office, they had my whole day filled with client and partner activities before I arrived, ensuring I always left town exhausted.

On these trips I learned that our new salesperson made incredibly polished presentations. I felt a bit intimidated when I presented in front of him because I knew he could do it better. But he didn't make me feel that way—he was genuinely appreciative and respectful.

Our Minneapolis team continued their grueling pace for about eleven months. They landed a few accounts, but their expectations were higher than most and a sense of desperation started to set in. The technical person was soon recruited away by a large company, which left the sales person to go it alone. He was feeling abandoned after his partner left and asked me for the secret to our other salespersons' successes. I told him, "You have to know in your heart with absolute certainty that you're going to succeed no matter what. Our highest achieving salespeople all went through a struggle with doubt. All those who decided they would succeed no matter what, made it. This holds true for anything you set out to accomplish in life."

About a month later the salesperson called me, wanting to resign. "Dan, I spent a lot of time thinking about our conversation," he said. "I want to believe that I will succeed no matter what, but the reality is I don't." I hated to see this team leave OST—I believed they were made for the company. Still do. But relentless determination means refusing to settle for anything less than total victory.

Pay It Square

About three years ago, one of our employees approached me with a business opportunity. He and a friend had developed an app they called Pay It Square (payitsquare.com), which allows an individual to easily collect money over the Internet by credit card. For example, say you needed to collect money for your class reunion. You could simply use Pay It Square to create a web page that you would then share via email or social media so that the invited alumni could use a card to pay online.

Obviously, profitability required a high volume of transactions, but with seven billion people in the world, it was a compelling business opportunity. Pay It Square was already live and people were using it, but it needed refinement—more functionality and adequate capital to market it.

After careful consideration OST agreed to invest in enhancing and marketing the product in exchange for a majority interest. Immediately after closing on the deal, we put a team to work and concurrently built a business plan. The plan contained a timeline with software development tasks, marketing initiatives, and revenue goals. We had an aggressive nine-month gestational period, which seemed an appropriate time frame as this was our baby, with a minimum goal of ten thousand dollars in monthly revenue. If we didn't achieve our minimum goal, we agreed to abandon the project at the end of month nine.

Our Pay It Square team was amazing—high energy, creative, and aggressive. The developers improved the functionality of the application while the marketing team worked tirelessly to drive demand. We tried everything we could think of to push the momentum forward including social media advertising, local press, email blasts, face-to-face meetings with nonprofits, blogging, and many others. Despite our best efforts, we failed miserably in driving demand. At the end of nine months our monthly revenue was approximately one thousand dollars—well short of our ten-thousand-dollar goal. We were all devastated and wanted to continue but knew the decision we had made without emotion nine months earlier was the right course of action.

So we set aside our valiant efforts, and life moved on—until twelve months later when out of the blue Pay It Square began to grow again at about 20 percent per month. We hadn't touched the site, but as people became more Internet savvy, they began proactively looking for applications to collect money. After a year and a half of inactivity, we started investing in Pay It Square again. This time our focus was entirely on the application itself. We wanted it to be attractive, function-rich, easy to use, and mobile friendly.

Since the site had jump-started itself we hoped it would continue to grow at a 20 percent clip for the foreseeable future—but it didn't. About two months into our development project the revenue slowed and actually started to slide. Disappointed and a bit confused, we refused to abandon the project this time around. There was such great potential here.

The development project lasted another nine months or so. We were pleased with the new look and feel, and apparently our clients were too because the numbers started to climb again. We eclipsed the magic ten thousand dollar monthly revenue number for the first time. Finally, it seemed to really be taking off—only to plateau around twelve thousand dollars a month. In our research we noticed that people were launching a lot of web pages to collect money, but only 10 to 20 percent of them were ever actually used. A little more analysis determined there were a few steps in our process that were too complicated and holding people up. So we tweaked. And we started investing again!

Now we all like happy endings, but unfortunately Pay It Square does not have a storybook ending—yet. We recently invested more into the site than ever before—and failed again. Sadly, we have decided to put Pay It Square on hold one more time. As an author I am tempted to tell you about all of our successes and conveniently ignore our failures. Unfortunately, the business world is tough and sometimes even the most relentless determination results in disappointment. So why do I tell you a story like this? We all experience failures in business, so don't be discouraged. Just dust yourself off and move on to the next initiative. If you continue to give your all, you will string together enough successes to have a thriving business or expand an already successful business.

To London

A few years ago, one of our clients requested that we open an overseas office in London. Most companies our size would have done the due diligence and decided against it. Opening an office in a different country creates complications that only billion-dollar companies with sophisticated finance organizations attempt.

Funny thing, though. It never occurred to us that our endeavor was too complicated or might fail. We just plunged ahead. The easiest parts of opening our London office were forming a limited corporation, establishing an address, and lining up our first employee. Our biggest challenges involved gaining authorization to sell HP, Cisco, and Dell products abroad and learning international finance and accounting rules and regulations, including the VAT tax.

Within six months we were up and running, taking orders, and shipping product. Our clients weren't surprised. After all this time they've come to expect we'll do what we say we'll do. Our vendors, on the other hand, were a bit shocked that a company as small as OST was able to pull this off—and they told us so.

You've probably been a part of or at least observed business cultures where every new endeavor gets picked apart as people point to all the reasons why it might fail. Call us naïve—or too good to be true, if you want—but our upbeat, confident attitude allows us to learn, grow, and flourish. That's why we can do things like open offices in foreign countries.

What Kirk Cousins Taught Us

Four years ago, NFL quarterback Kirk Cousins gave a motivational speech to our employees at OST. When Kirk arrived, we felt a little star struck but did our best to make him feel welcome and comfortable. A local hero and three-year starting QB at Michigan State University, Kirk quickly put us at ease. He asked us several questions and we could tell by his thoughtful interaction that he was a good and caring listener.

Kirk was the 102nd overall pick of the 2012 NFL draft by the Washington Redskins. His fellow quarterback Robert Griffin III turned out to be the 2011 Heisman Trophy winner, second over-all pick of the entire draft and was also recruited by the Redskins. Kirk's star had been temporarily eclipsed, and he was forced to become second-string.

But Kirk refused to succumb to the jealousy or frustration that might consume most of us. His speech at OST focused on the feelings he was having playing behind Griffin, known to his fans as RG3. Initially he viewed RG3 as his competitor for the starting spot and things didn't go so well. But then he made the conscious choice to be a winner, regardless of whether he ever started or not. Once Kirk decided to support RG3 and help him be the best he could be, everything changed. You see, Kirk has an unusual combination of strengths. He has raw determination and is also the consummate team player.

Kirk and RG3 became fast friends and learned to support each other. Whenever RG3 started as quarterback, Kirk did everything he could to make RG3 successful. When RG3 was injured and Kirk started, RG3 was there as a source of support for Kirk.

Kirk started at quarterback for the Redskins for three seasons before signing the largest guaranteed contract in NFL history with the Minnesota Vikings in 2018. His story is the definition of relentless determination.

The most wildly successful business cultures are born when everyone is driven to succeed and everyone has each other's back.

We can all learn from Kirk's thought process and actions. After all, Kirk is now the starting quarterback for the Washington Redskins.

So What Does This Mean to You?

Does your business culture thrive on challenges? Do you possess that relentless determination to succeed no matter what? What game-changing business initiative have you been avoiding because you think you might not have what it takes to make it work?

If you're willing to push through every obstacle, this kind of contagious persistence will transform your culture and your business. Consider placing tenacity as one of the primary traits you look for when recruiting.

Few but Powerful

How (and How Not) to Form a Limited Number of Highly Valuable Partnerships

CHAPTER THEME SONG:
"ALL YOU NEED IS LOVE," JOHN LENNON

In the mideighties I was on IBM's subcontract procurement team in Poughkeepsie, New York, specializing in the negotiation of multimillion-dollar contracts. My team members and I were all trained by the Chester Karrass School of negotiations combined with IBM internal instruction. Our manager, a charismatic leader, called us the Green Berets, and we truly believed we were the best.

One particular negotiation stands out. We were hammering out a large contract with a New York–based vendor to assemble a portion of our 3080 mainframe computers. (We had different vendors assemble different "frames," preventing any one vendor from possessing the capability to build the whole machine.) The best word to describe these negotiations was brutal because both sides wanted to win.

At age twenty-six I was the lead IBM negotiator, and we were negotiating against a team of seasoned veterans. Our team consisted of a manufacturing engineer, a quality engineer, an industrial engineer, a finance specialist, and a senior procurement specialist (that was me). The median age on our team was somewhere close to twenty-seven. The median age of our competition was closer to forty-five.

We decided to use the classic good-guy/bad-guy approach we had learned in school but had never executed in a real situation. Our preparation for the negotiation was critical to our success, and we spent several hours role playing and strategizing. Because I was understood by the customer to be a person who was pleasant and easy to get along with, we decided I should be the bad guy. Our rationale was simple: if I blew up during the negotiation, it would shock them into giving us the price we wanted.

On negotiation day our team was a bundle of nerves, but we did our best not to show it. We had all studied the numbers from every angle imaginable and felt confident they could do nothing to confuse us or take us off track.

We waited until the second day of the negotiation to throw our plan into action. Gradually I pretended to become more and more frustrated and unhappy throughout the day. Then finally it was show time! I blew up and shouted, "I can't believe what I am hearing! This is crazy; you guys are not budging and are way over-priced! This is ridiculous! This is the maximum we are willing to pay!" And I stormed out of the room. Truth be told, I was not upset in the slightest, but I could tell by the looks on their faces that my performance had the desired effect.

About an hour later I received a phone call at my desk from the assembly vendor's lead negotiator. "Dan, I am so sorry . . . we did not mean to offend you. We are agreeable with the number you gave us. Can we shake hands and call it a deal?" As I agreed to the terms and conditions, I remember doing my best to sound like a tough guy so they would not know it was all an act. We were all so proud of our big win, I told the story over and over again to my peers to impress them. Considering my acting ability, I was probably so bad they didn't know what to think. It felt like Mr. Rogers vs. Mark Cuban!

Even as I write this, my stomach knots and my pulse quickens.

I'm embarrassed and somewhat ashamed to tell this story. This negotiation, though successful in the short run, destroyed any trust we had with the assembly vendor and made doing business with them miserable for both of us. I'm certain this vendor was able to beat us in any future negotiations. So ultimately, we learned to play a game where no one wins. I learned that what I did that day was the antithesis of building a trusting partnership.

I should have apologized then or maybe now if I could remember the names of the people from thirty years ago. I know the chances are slim to none that they are reading this book, but if you are I want to say that I am sorry.

The Makings of a Powerful Partnership

During the first few years at OST we built a partnership with Crowe Chizek, a local accounting and consulting firm. They were a large regional player that sold software to run manufacturing and distribution companies. Crowe Chizek built a team of over a hundred experts on software but felt their clients would be better served with an additional partner selling the hardware that ran the application programs. We had several meetings before we decided to work together as a team. Crowe Chizek would sell and implement the software, and OST would do the same with the hardware.

Crowe Chizek, or Crowe Horwath as the company is now known, taught OST the true meaning of partnership. It is the model we use today. Once we agreed to partner with Crowe, we established a document that clearly defined the roles and responsibilities of each company. Crowe taught us that it was important for everyone to understand exactly how the partnership was going to work.

Establishing structure was important, but the key to success was the attitude each partner brought to the table. In order for a partnership to be successful, each party must look for ways to advance their partner's interests without thinking about what they are getting in return. Ninety-nine percent of partnerships don't work this way. Companies and individuals are focused too much on what's in it for them. These partnerships remain lukewarm at best.

Crowe set the bar. We were in the partnership for about six months when it became clear I was providing the sales and implementation support Crowe was looking for, but the customers were not buying their hardware from me. When the Crowe team became aware of this, they invited me to a meeting with the primary players in their practice—including the sales people. I remember being intimidated by the caliber of the people and their high degree of professionalism.

In this meeting they decided to include my hardware in every Crowe proposal going forward. As a result, my win rate went from two out of every ten deals to eight out of ten. It wasn't long before OST followed suit, and a powerful partnership took shape. Crowe would do anything for OST, and OST would do anything for Crowe. It was a winning combination that lasted for many years. In fact, we still do business with Crowe today.

Selective but Generous

It's great to showcase a stellar partnership like the one we just shared, but it seems like partnerships have become too plentiful. Everyone wants to partner with everyone else—good in theory, but poor in practice. In some ways it has become almost meaningless to say you have a partnership with another company because everyone else is a partner with them too.

At OST partnerships have been critical to our culture and business success, and we take them seriously. Our goal is to be considered the ultimate partner by our clients, vendors, distributors, and peer companies. We have several clients with whom we enjoy wonderful partnerships, even ones we're not sure we deserve at times. One particular client has stuck with us through thick and thin: Metro Health. They are a progressive community hospital that takes pride in being on the far edge of the technology curve, atypical for a small hospital. We have worked with Metro for over ten years, and our mutual trust has grown immensely. We would do anything for them and they treat us the same way.

A few years back, Metro pioneered a Virtual Desktop Infrastructure (VDI) before anyone knew what VDI was. In the likely case you've never heard of VDI, just think of it as technology that saves doctors and nurses significant time on their jobs allowing them to spend more time with patients. VDI was transformational for Metro Health and literally put them on the national map. They were featured in numerous publications and case studies. But the technology was so leading edge, implementing it slowed their entire system to a crawl for several days.

Metro could have fired us as a vendor for the delays resulting from implementing the system, but because of their past experience with OST, they put their trust in us. When all was said and done, Metro Health CIO Bill Lewkowski said, "I am speechless. From what was a disaster to what has become a miracle, I am grateful and indebted to such dedication, service, and excellence! You all rose to the challenge and found a way to save our situation. I want to thank OST for your true partnership. I was without words. All I can say is that I'm grateful to work side by side with such a team. You guys are part of what makes Metro special."

This is the kind of partnership that lasts. Statements like the one above from a client go a long way; you can imagine that we pull out all the stops when it comes to Metro Health—when they say jump, we say, how high.

Making First Meetings Count

We all know the drill when it comes to first meetings with vendor companies that want to partner. The company that initiates the meeting performs the Macarena, presenting their company overview and what it is they're hoping you'll sell on their behalf. They listen to what you have to say and miraculously decide that your company is the ideal fit for jointly selling their product and/or service—then they shower you with the benefits you'll gain from working with them. In addition to the margins you'll make on their product or service, they usually commit to bringing you into other high-value client accounts because of your unique skill set.

They mean well typically, but the likelihood of them actually bringing you into those other accounts is on par with the odds of an Eskimo meeting a snake charmer at an ear-pulling contest. Quite often the person who's making the commitment is either a business development person or an executive and does not have the authority or the client relationship to bring you into an account. The sales people control *who* is introduced into their accounts, and they rarely see things the same way as the business development people and executives. Both parties agree to be BFFs and conquer the world together, but nothing comes of it.

I prefer to lay everything on the table: "Hey guys, I've been in hundreds of these meetings and I am sure that you have to. We all have the best of intentions and feel good about our new partnership right now, but our priorities—with all likelihood—change as soon as we walk back into our hectic tyranny-of-the-urgent business lives. OST partners with a few select vendors and those relationships run deep. We have an interest in partnering with you but require a level of commitment on your end to move to the next step. Here's what we propose: If you'll bring us into four new opportunities, we promise to give it our all. Do you have four opportunities that might benefit from our involvement?" I also go on to explain the kind of partner we will be if we make it to the next step. This overall approach saves a good deal of time and energy for both parties. Simply put, if the vendor is not willing to bring you into four accounts, they must not want you as much as they say they do.

How you treat your partners has a direct effect on your culture and your reputation in the marketplace. Your employees see how you talk about partners internally and how you treat them externally. If your cultural emphasis is on your employees and their families, but you treat your partners with disrespect, your employees will be confused by this inconsistency. Likewise, if you aren't fair in your dealings with your partners, the community will find out quickly and it's sure to taint how other companies regard you.

Selective World-Class Service

At OST we limit the number of partners we do business with, choose them carefully, treat them with the utmost care and respect, and do everything we can to help them be successful. Experience tells us that continually keeping each partner's best interests in mind and giving of ourselves without "keeping score" is the best way to go. In most cases the partners we choose see our approach and act accordingly. Occasionally we pick a partner that doesn't get it, and soon after we find ourselves reevaluating the relationship.

If you are choosy about which companies you partner with, limit the number of partnerships, and give unconditionally to each of them, your culture will benefit. So it's important to develop your own "partnership filter" by establishing the criteria of companies that you want to do business with and what you will do to treat them well. Ultimately, you want your partners to feel like they've won the lottery when they do business with you. They win, you win, and your culture thrives.

So What Does This Mean to You?

When having first meetings with potential partners, be direct in your approach. Explain what you are looking for in the partnership and test how serious they are by requesting them to take an action—not just words.

Consider limiting the number of business partnerships that you have and concentrating your efforts on those that are most important to your business. Too many partnerships dilute the effectiveness of those that are critical to your business. Formalizing your key partnerships with documented clearly defined roles and responsibilities often brings partnerships to a new level. Spend less energy thinking about what you are looking for in the partnership and more time thinking about what you can do for your partner. Ultimately the amount of effort you each put into the partnership will determine the level of success.

PART FOUR

STAYING RELEVANT

Innovation and Marketing

Overcoming
Silver Lake Syndrome

Innovation in a World of Naysayers

CHAPTER THEME SONG:
"THE GAMBLER," KENNY ROGERS

Over twenty years ago my family and I were tent camping with my wife's parents. The second night it rained so hard our tent began flooding. Our seven-year-old son Kyle was in the wrong spot at the wrong time and got soaked. When we woke up the next morning and it was still raining, everyone was irritable and cranky.

As we packed up camp, the sun came out and my father-in-law, Fred, suggested we stop by the Silver Lake State Park on our way home to go swimming. He likes taking his time on the back roads, which we affectionately call "Fred drives" to this day. So he pointed, in a Fred sort of way, and we were off. It wasn't long before we suspected we might be lost and realized Fred was simply "feeling" his way around. (Keep in mind this was before smart phones and GPS were the navigational norm.)

When I look back now, it seems like the directions were straight forward enough, but somehow, I got mixed up. As we approached the general Silver Lake vicinity, I must have taken a right turn when

I should have taken a left. We followed the road to the end and turned around in a cul-de-sac. As I was pulling out of the turn, I noticed a "For Sale" sign on my right.

Four tumbledown cottages stared back at me along the most beautiful sugar-sand beach I had ever seen. We pulled off to the side of the road to take a closer look. Sure enough, all four of the cottages were for sale on one piece of property. So now my head started spinning with what ifs. "What if we could find a way to buy one of these places? What if the asking price was too high? What if we couldn't come up with the money? What if we could convince friends and family to buy the cottages with us?"

I did some quick mental math. We guessed that the asking price for the property would be somewhere around $200,000, which would make the individual purchase prices approximately $50,000 each. Hmmm . . . $50,000 was more than we could afford for a summer place. Of course, at that point $50 was probably more than we could afford. As I maneuvered through these mental gymnastics, I was feeling a little deflated, but not willing to give up just yet. We decided to move on to the state park and go for that swim. Everyone had a great time, which made us all feel markedly better about the rainy camping weekend.

In typical OCD (obsessive compulsive Dan) fashion, my mind had already raced ahead, and the next day I called to find out how much they were asking for the entire property. I was shocked at how low it was—$130,000! It seemed too good to be true. My wife, Barb, and I had several discussions about how we might make this work. Practically speaking, we would need to convince three other families to purchase cottages for us to afford one. I checked with a real estate attorney about creating a condominium agreement and was told that we could do this at a relatively low cost. So we made a decision to purchase the property—but only if we could search out some other buyers.

We made a list of friends and family who we thought might be interested and started contacting them. I was so enthusiastic, I was telling everyone at work, at church, in the neighborhood, and everywhere I went about my grand plans. As a wildly optimistic person, I expected some pushback, but the negative reactions from most people truly surprised me. They would politely listen to me describe the cottages and my hope of finding three other buyers. Then they pointed out all the things that would doubtlessly go wrong. Many of them insisted there was no way four families could get along owning property like this together. They questioned how we would decide on which family gets which cottage. They predicted that the huge sand dune at the end of the road would eventually cover the cottages. In the end they all insisted there was just too much risk.

Not surprisingly, such negativity did not deter me, but it seemed strange that so many people would feel this way. Nevertheless, I eventually convinced three families to "buy in," and they became as excited about the project as we were. Together we offered $110,000 for all four cottages and the owner accepted our offer! We were able to purchase our waterfront cottage for $23,500 and embark on a lifelong adventure, all because we got lost and took a little time out to enjoy the ride.

Over twenty years later my grown children claim Silver Lake as one of their favorite places in the world, and I know it's one of the best decisions we've ever made for our family. We consider the other cottage owners some of our very best friends and look forward to spending time around the campfire with them every summer.

Weaving Innovation into Culture

My Silver Lake experience taught me a valuable lesson about innovation. Many people don't know how to handle ideas that are out of the ordinary. In other words, if they're processing an idea and don't have a personal experience close enough to draw a parallel, they reject the idea. This isn't exactly surprising or even exceptional, really. It's fairly normal human behavior. I call it "Silver Lake Syndrome" and believe understanding it has been a critical part of my success in leading OST.

Our commitment to innovation differentiates OST from its competitors. Most information technology companies ask their customers what projects they have going on. OST asks its customers what we can do to transform their businesses.

As an entrepreneurial company dependent on innovative ideas to compete, OST team members generate dozens of "what if" ideas across the company every day. There is naturally a significant amount of healthy pushback on these ideas. Every company needs to find the right balance of innovative risk that best fits their culture. When I hear someone pushing back on an innovative idea, I don't get defensive the way I might have before Silver Lake. I listen, and I try to figure out if their pushback is rational and well-reasoned or if it's the result of their own limitations or inexperience.

This more sensitive approach has allowed us to become increasingly innovative over time . . . and has become one of the hallmarks of our culture. We take pride in the imaginative ways we approach all areas of our business. As a result, we've explored areas of new technology we might have resisted if we didn't understand the psychology of out-of-the-box (or "into-the-cottage") thinking.

We have been told by consultants that OST has an unusual breadth of technical expertise for a company of our size. In recent years we have been finding ways to leverage this by bringing innovation to our clients that other companies our size cannot—and that larger companies are too lethargic to deliver in a timely, cost-effective manner.

In fact, OST's wide-ranging set of competencies combines the complementary capabilities of our application development, business process, managed service, and data center groups, with the assistance of our project management office allowing us to truly and demonstrably transform our clients' businesses.

We even changed our traditional chief technology officer's title to chief innovation officer—now that's commitment to radical thinking! We understand the natural human tendency to push back on innovation, but we also see the enormous value of innovation as a competitive tool in a high-pressure, low-risk tolerance business world. We have found that even our tried-and-true clients are not immune to Silver Lake Syndrome. So we take it slow and allow them time to sort out our innovative ideas. But we do not give up when we see a little pushback.

How Elon Musk Does It

Innovation, by definition, is new and unfamiliar—and therefore uncomfortable for many people. When Morse, Edison, and Ford invented new devices, they were often misunderstood and under-estimated. Now, of course, their names have become synonymous with these innovative contributions.

Similarly, technology has advanced thanks to pioneers like Bill Gates and Steve Jobs. One of my personal heroes of innova-tion, Elon Musk, continues to change the world as we know it. His building blocks are the result of past innovators, but he consistently pushes technologies to incredible levels of excellence we could not have imagined a decade ago.

Musk serves as the CEO, CTO, and cofounder of SpaceX (Space Exploration Technologies), which designs, manufactures, and launches advanced rockets and spacecraft. Its goals are refresh-ingly audacious as evidenced by matter-of-fact statements like this one on the SpaceX website: "The company was founded in 2002 to revolutionize space technology, with the ultimate goal of enabling people to live on other planets." Besides Captain Kirk, who makes those kinds of statements?

Elon Musk does, and he is dead serious. "The key thing for me," he begins, "is to develop the technology to transport large numbers of people and cargo to Mars. That's the ultimate awesome thing." Musk envisions a colony with eighty thousand people on the red planet."[1]

Space travel isn't his only passion. For getting around here on planet Earth, Musk developed Tesla Motors, designing the best-rated

1 Rory Carroll, "Elon Musk's Mission to Mars," *The Guardian*, July 17, 2013.

car ever produced in automobile history—and it just happens to be electric. *Consumers Reports* gave the Tesla S a score of 99 out of 100, the highest score awarded to any car tested. Unbelievable for a car company that had only been in existence for a dozen years!

Tesla is now determined to build the ultimate electric car battery and plans to open the world's largest electric car battery plant soon. Elon Musk predicts that the new factory will produce batteries for 500,000 vehicles by 2020. In addition, Tesla recently turned the industry upside down by making their design secrets open to the public. In June 2014 Tesla removed all their patents and made them open source!

As if SpaceX and Tesla are not enough, Elon Musk's latest highly publicized idea is a high-speed transportation system known as the Hyperloop. Think of climbing into a tube, like the ones you see at a bank drive-through (only slightly larger) and being transported at eight hundred miles per hour from San Francisco to Los Angeles in thirty minutes. Yep, there's much more to come from Elon Musk. He's only forty-three!

You Can Change the World

Elon Musk must have learned his way around the Silver Lake Syndrome at an early age because he was obviously not dissuaded by naysayers. Can you imagine what people must have said when Musk shared his desire to start a company with the ultimate goal of enabling people to live on other planets? "What planet are *you* on?" was surely one of them!

Perhaps you're falling victim to a little Silver Lake Syndrome thinking yourself about now. "Sure, Elon Musk may change the world, but he's a genius with billions of dollars. I don't have those kinds of resources or abilities. I can't change the world."

Wrong.

How will this world ever change for the better if you and I don't dare to dream big?

At OST we have the courage to believe we can change the world. It is possible we'll make our mark in technology, but our best bet is developing groundbreaking business culture concepts that can be replicated by others. Our culture is healthy, but we have much bigger things in mind: the ultimate work place where everyone is understood, thrives, and becomes the best they can be, both personally and professionally.

What big ideas do you have? Ignore the naysayers and you might just find yourself leading your industry or in a cottage by the lake!

So What Does This Mean to You?

The next time someone approaches you with an extraordinary idea, take a breath. Don't shoot anything down without first exploring the possibilities. The next time you come up with an idea that requires overcoming the odds, don't let anyone easily talk you out of it. Put your stake in the ground.

Regardless of the industry you are in and your level of risk tolerance, make room for at least some innovation. If your company is known for being innovative, learn from Elon Musk, and set an audacious goal. Then go after it with everything you've got!

It's Addictive

Entrepreneurial Spirit

CHAPTER THEME SONG:
"I WANT A NEW DRUG," HUEY LEWIS AND THE NEWS

We have always encouraged our employees to start new business practices that we call "businesses within a business." This is one of the primary reasons we have been successful in growing organically with over 30 percent compounded annual growth for eleven years. It's also one of the many reasons professionals choose to join OST and what keeps them engaged and interested over the long haul.

A couple years ago we decided to take our entrepreneurial support to a whole new level. OST now allows our employees to run their own businesses on the side and encourages them to consider partnering with us to bring those ideas to market as reflected in this announcement to our employees:

> We would like to encourage all of you to come forward with ideas for intellectual property (IP) at OST. We would also like to see you benefit financially when you share the idea and participate in developing the product or service during hours outside of OST. For example, we recently had an employee approach us with a mobile application that he had developed for a GPS activated garage door opener. We are considering an arrangement where OST

brings the product to market and the employee maintains a percentage of ownership.

As little as three years ago I would have been the first to fight against employees developing products on the side. As a matter of fact, we prohibited them from doing so in their employment agreements.

Over time, though, our thinking evolved. We recognized an opportunity to add something unique and valuable to our ever-evolving culture. We thought, technology people are natural problem solvers so let's provide them with an innovation outlet. Instead of this creative energy potentially causing conflict with their work schedule and employment agreement, we wanted to become facilitators and catalysts for innovation.

We saw many potential positive outcomes:

1. Employees become even more energized doing their everyday work.
2. Employees gain knowledge that is transferable to assisting our clients.
3. Employees are contented in their careers with OST.
4. If employees are highly successful in bringing a product or service to market, it may result in another highly productive employer in our community.

Open-Me

Let's look at a venture that we pursued with an employee—the GPS-activated garage door opener. Justin Menkveld developed the prototype of an app and associated hardware that allows someone to open and close their garage door, from anywhere in the world, with a simple click on their cell phone. It can also open their garage door automatically when they arrive home and close it when they leave.

Justin approached OST to gauge our interest in jointly marketing the product and fine-tuning it for mass production. We were highly interested and signed a Letter of Understanding with Justin within weeks. We named the product Open-Me and decided to launch it on Kickstarter.

We agreed to work with our patent attorney to make sure existing patents were not violated, to partner with a local manufacturer to get estimated pricing and timelines for designing and manufacturing the hardware component of the product, to develop a high-end video describing the product, to assign an OST business development person to be responsible for execution, and to create a high-quality Kickstarter page.

A few months later we launched Open-Me on Kickstarter and waited for the orders to start rolling in. They didn't! We scrambled—put our best people on it, asked for help from our employees, called out favors from our social media acquaintances, contacted friends and family, and pleaded with business partners and bloggers. In the end the orders were one tenth of what we expected, even after our last-minute mad dash to generate orders. The agony of defeat was disheartening.

What did we learn? We were overconfident and underestimated the value of having previous experience with launching products on Kickstarter. We didn't have a social media strategy or any sort of social media following before we launched. We set an unrealistic sales goal that was way too high. We had several people at OST reaching out to friends and family asking them to pledge but learned that it's better if the request comes directly from the inventor. The campaign should've been more personal—more about Justin and less about Open-Me. That's what this entrepreneurial stuff is all about . . . learning from our mistakes.

So what happened next? Since we were unsuccessful in raising the funds needed to launch Open-Me, OST gave one hundred percent of the ownership back to Justin along with all of the materials we had created. In return, Justin agreed to pay our costs back if the product was successful in the future.

Justin was not willing to give up and has taken a second shot at developing and marketing Open-Me on his own. He released the prototype product and it was impressive. Justin is on to other things now, but he is one of those entrepreneurs who will eventually succeed—he clearly has what it takes.

Advice to Entrepreneurs (and Business Leaders with Entrepreneurial Businesses)

This is how great business people are made. After you have fought through ten thousand roadblocks you become a master at getting things done. You learn to view challenges as both invigorating and fun. It takes a special kind of person to be a successful entrepreneur, and OST is full of them, all at varying stages of their journey. People often ask me how to take an idea and turn it into a successful business or new businesses within their existing business. I assure them that they will run into obstacles, but regardless of what stands in their way, they need to trust, to know with complete certainty, that they'll succeed. Each time something blocks your path, you need to power through it, tunnel under it, go around it, or leap over it and then be prepared for the next something.

After all that—when everything is said and done—your chances of success are still only about 20 percent or so, even for a new business venture within an existing business. Yes, you heard me right: the odds are 20 percent success, but you must be 100 hundred percent certain you will succeed. Every time.

So What Does This Mean to You?

Even if your company would not be considered entrepreneurial today, in the beginning it had to be; after all, someone had to start the company. Think about how introducing more entrepreneurially minded projects within your company will make your people more passionate about their jobs. You might even consider encouraging your employees to do start-ups on the side like we do at OST; although, that might be a stretch for many industries.

If you do launch an entrepreneurial product or services campaign within your company, think of it like a fun game and view the roadblocks as interesting challenges.

CEOs, Costa Rica, and Corvettes

The Wonder of What If?

CHAPTER THEME SONG:
"UP ON THE ROOF," JAMES TAYLOR

Inspiration crops up in all kinds of unexpected places. Several years ago, my wife, Barb, and I attended an inspiring Ernst & Young Entrepreneur of the Year event in Palm Springs. It was way over the top—in a good way. This was a "Presidents and CEOs only" affair with over a thousand in attendance, not including participants' significant others. And these were no ordinary CEOs. I was running a good-sized company, but most of these people led companies much larger both in size and revenue than OST.

While the Palm Springs event is only one small part of Ernst & Young's amazing Entrepreneur of the Year program, what a part it is! Exquisite food, dynamic speakers, A-list entertainment, and attention to the smallest of details exceeding anything I had ever experienced. The speakers included Troy Aikman, Francis Ford Coppola, Wayne Gretzky, Michael Dell, Mia Hamm, Herbert Kohler Jr., Magic Johnson, and President George W. Bush. Performing separate greatest hits concerts, the Beach Boys and the Eagles dazzled us.

This commitment to excellence had the power to bring this many CEOs together—along with the exceptional opportunity to get to know each other and exchange ideas.

Dreaming Big

When I returned to Earth, er, Michigan, I couldn't get this fabulous gathering out of my head. I kept asking myself, "There must be a way I can use this same concept to host a minievent for OST. There is huge value in doing business at the CEO level, but we did not have relationships with many of the CEOs at the largest companies in our area. Maybe the place to start is with motivation and outcome? Ernst & Young is obviously passionate about its Entrepreneur of the Year program and wants to stimulate, inspire, and celebrate its lucky participants. So what am I most passionate about? Who do I want to impact in a similar way?"

The answer was easy. Beyond the OST family I love my alma mater, Michigan State University, and my community of West Michigan. With the Ernst & Young event in mind, I decided to host a CEO event of my own—the largest companies from the area who claimed Michigan State alumni as their CEOs.

I was delighted to find that many of the CEOs of the largest multibillion-dollar companies in West Michigan were, in fact, Michigan State graduates. As proud and excited as I felt upon this discovery, it also intimidated me. What if I invited these power players to an event . . . and no one came? What if they came . . . and it flatlined? What if I had spinach in my teeth the whole evening . . . and no one told me? Actually, my wife is great at food in the teeth surveillance, so that last one was never a real concern, but you get the picture. Well, after a lot of thought, I decided to throw my fears aside and go for it.

I assumed these CEOs ran in the same circles, but surely a few of them wouldn't know each other. Meeting and mingling might be a strong incentive for them to come. Even if they were already acquainted, getting the entire group together at once would be enjoyable, right? Go Green! Hosted by OST, we wanted the event to reflect our personality and style, so we kept our invitation lighthearted:

> No fundraising here, so leave your checkbook at home. This gathering is all about celebrating our common Spartan bond in an easy, relaxed environment. Getting to know one another and enjoying a remarkable meal together. After attending an Ernst & Young CEO event in Palm Springs last fall, Dan Behm (president of OST), decided it would be fun to host a mini-CEO event in Grand Rapids for Michigan State University graduates. No specific agenda . . . other than having a great time and promoting MSU. The event will be held in OST's homey (not homely) offices, featuring a fifteen-hundred-square-foot kitchen.

Mike Lomonaco, OST director of marketing, knew one of the CEOs on our list personally, so he worked with him to gain credibility. We contacted every CEO by email, with a personal phone call, and then had the invitations hand delivered. In all, nine CEOs and their spouses were asked to attend. They all made it, and we had an awesome time together!

In addition to hiring a top chef for the evening, we invited MSU basketball star Steve Smith as our special guest. We also had a couple surprises planned . . . to make sure no one would leave disappointed. Mateen Cleaves, an MSU basketball star from the 2000 championship team, attended, and the Discords, the MSU men's a cappella group, entertained us during our dinner's own "half time." The smoked salmon and beef Carpaccio delighted our palates, while the a cappella group sounded amazing and wowed us with music and humor throughout the evening. We've enjoyed four CEO events so far and hope to have many more. Pure OST in my book.

You don't need to know celebrity athletes and rock stars to host this kind of forum for building community among leaders. What standout event could you host that leverages your passion and challenges your imagination? What are the things that have earned your devotion? Certainly, a few others in your community, your personal life, or business life share your excitement for _____. Just imagine what it might be like to get this group of people together and rally around these interests.

Let's say, for example, you know three community leaders who could learn from one another, who just happen to share your love of red wine. And your love of sailing. Just not at the same time! If you organized a wine tasting event for the four of you with Ben Ainslie—sailor and Olympic champion—as a special guest, do you think they would come? Heck, I would! Start planning your event today and make shared passion the focus! You can't lose.

OST Considers New Location . . . in Costa Rica!

One key to balancing creativity and process comes from the cultural freedom to speak up and throw out new ideas. Process reliance often plateaus into boredom and lowers morale because no one feels free to question the status quo or offer new ideas. Similarly, with permission to speak freely ingrained in your culture, people can hold one another accountable and make sure that creative focus doesn't totally compromise the process. Every time I announce I have a new idea, OST staffers roll their eyes. "Oh no! What now?" But I think they really like it—most of the time!

Sometimes it's the outrageous-sounding ideas that have the most impact. One of our leadership team's more interesting brainstorms was to purchase a resort in Costa Rica to provide our employees and their families a memorable, nonconventional work experience. Yes, seriously.

This arguably extreme idea never made the final cut—we decided against it shortly after our accountant regained consciousness—so why bother to mention it? Because, it is this kind of outrageous idea that make dramatic changes to your culture.

We looked seriously into acquiring El Castillo Boutique Luxury Hotel in Ojochal, Costa Rica. The idea was to give all our employees the opportunity to work in Costa Rica for three weeks, every third year. They would also be given the option to take one of those three weeks as a vacation week. OST would provide accommodations at no charge. The employees would just be responsible for the cost of airfare. We wanted to include airfare too, but that really threw a wrench into the numbers. Surprisingly, the cost to provide this benefit to our employees (without the airfare) was much lower than what you might expect, especially considering the potential upside. Tan employees are happy employees!

A retreat like this can provide valuable opportunities for your staff members and their families. Talk about an employee mixer! Deepening relationships in a fabulous, exotic setting is a great perk. This is also an experience that many might not be able to afford on their own. Such an incentive would doubtlessly sweeten the deal when it comes to hiring and retention. Considered from all angles, the idea is really not as crazy as it sounds!

Now, you might be thinking, "If the cost is so reasonable, why isn't everyone doing this?" My theory, which I shared earlier, is that people naturally catalog all the obstacles . . . and talk themselves right out of it. What if we purchase the resort and no one uses it? What if some families can't afford the airfare and they become resentful because others are using the resort while they can't? What about families with children in school; surely, they can't arrange for three weeks away? What if an employee or family member is injured; isn't this a huge liability for our company? Won't the scheduling be a nightmare? And on and on.

Can't, isn't, won't. Listen, anything unique and worth doing is going to be a challenge, but why let that stop you? Can you imagine how over the moon your employees would be if you introduced a program like this? Do you think they'd be more loyal to your company? Do you think they would tell others about the amazing place they work? Do you think the relationships they'd build with the other families would result in better teamwork and company-wide relationships? If you answered yes to all of the above, consider tailoring this idea to something that might work for your company.

Brainstorming Our Way to Corvettes

Playing with new ideas is the lifeblood of creativity in a healthy culture. Regular "what if?" sessions provide a great way to generate innovative ideas—the yin to that process yang.

We use a brainstorming methodology at OST that is easy, entertaining, and effective. It works so well, in fact, I've used it with at least three organizations outside of OST yielding extraordinary results. I will describe our process by telling you about one particular OST session that stands out in my mind.

First, we identify a difficulty to be solved or a goal we want to reach. In this case we had a business problem we were trying to remedy. We were aware of a few large accounts in our area that we were confident would benefit from our technical expertise, but they refused to meet with us. This is not unusual in the sales world, and companies like ours covet the chance to meet with good prospective clients. Truth is, most companies that accept a first meeting with OST request a second meeting and usually do business with us in time. So we decided to hold a brainstorming session with this mandate: "Come up with a foolproof way to ensure meetings with six targeted accounts."

We chose eight OST employees to participate in this exercise, which was scheduled for two hours in one of our conference rooms. We explained the rules to those unfamiliar with our methodology. We would start with one person and then go around the room asking each of them for their idea. We would continue to go around the table—over and over—until we reached at least one hundred ideas. While we were brainstorming, there was no such thing as a bad idea.

The first few rounds of ideas were simple and expected. As the session went on, maybe fifty to sixty responses later, I could see the strain on people's faces. Sensible ideas began to dry up. Participants began to get more and more crazy with their outside-the-box thinking as we closed in on one hundred suggestions. But it was at this point that the most innovative possibilities emerged.

As we reached the midnineties, an idea surfaced to captivate us all: send a Corvette key to the CIO of each company. The Corvette key would be accompanied by a note requesting a half hour introductory meeting—along with a promise to deliver a Corvette on the day of the meeting that the CIO could drive for a week. Even if a particular CIO was not overly excited about driving the Corvette for a week, we felt there was a chance they would see the idea as so off-the-wall they would agree to the meeting—if for no other reason than to meet those jokers from OST! We have yet to execute this idea, but we remain committed to giving it a shot. I just know it's going to work!

Finding Your Balance

Every company needs to strike a balance between creativity and process. Companies that rely exclusively on the latter are often efficient and methodical but run an enormous risk of burnout, stagnation, and cultural boredom. Companies that run chiefly on the fuel of the former may indeed nurture a dynamic culture but suffer from disorganization, missed opportunities, and starry-eyed risk taking. When the two hit that harmonious sweet spot together, your company is sure to outshine the competition.

Even if your company appears balanced and employees are thriving, I recommend cultivating a culture of self-reflection and idea generation as I've outlined here. Demonstrating your team's commitment to open communication to honor both creativity and process will provide stability and help sustain growth. In other words, don't be too quick to dismiss someone's idea about driving a new Corvette to that corporate retreat center in Costa Rica!

So What Does This Mean to You?

Take action and host an event playing off the ideas from the Ernst & Young and OST MSU CEO events. Not only will you have fun, but you will be providing others the opportunity to connect with individuals who share similar passions and provide you with the ultimate networking experience.

Put your own twist on the Costa Rica idea and explore the possibilities. Maybe a condo in Manhattan near the theater district, maybe a company membership at a spa resort, maybe an annual company cruise—the possibilities are truly endless.

I also encourage you to experiment with a "What if?" session of your own. The optimal group size for our brainstorming methodology is six or eight, but it'll work with fewer folks or a few more. It's best to select a group of people with different backgrounds as much as possible. OST sessions with the best results included participants who were creative, engaged, and truly motivated to come up with an optimal creative solution. Most of the best ideas come near the end of the session—after all the conventional ideas have been exhausted.

One possibility is to focus a brainstorming session on ways to find and maintain harmony between process and creativity. Striking this balance between the two will infuse your culture with the order and security needed to function efficiently, as well as the spontaneity and experimentation that make work enjoyable and often unpredictable.

You might start by simply assessing which one—creativity or process—your organization presently tilts toward. I'd encourage you to consider which one is your company's leaning by default. When things get stressful, do team members become more rigid and process oriented? Or is the mood more chaotic as individuals search for creative solutions?

....(19)...

What's with the Head?

How We Completely Rebranded Our Website

CHAPTER THEME SONG:
"THE TIMES THEY ARE A-CHANGIN'," BOB DYLAN

About nine years ago we decided to revamp our company website at ostusa.com. This is when we introduced the OST head as an attention grabber and memory stamp. I remember revealing the head at our annual company kickoff meeting. I was so proud of it and thought everyone would love it—they didn't. It made about a third of the people feel uncomfortable.

I could have dropped the head right then and there (not literally), but I didn't. My instincts told me to keep it, and boy am I glad that I did. "The head" and OST went together like peas and carrots, though today we use it selectively in our marketing campaigns to draw attention to key aspects of our story.

The OST Head

What's in a Website?

Our website is often a person's first encounter with OST. So when we revamped our site we needed our message to be clear and compelling—to reflect who we really are, to emphasize the importance of our company's culture, to identify what we have to offer our clients, and to be memorable. It was easy to describe what we wanted to do with our website, but it took an enormous amount of hard work, energy, and many reiterations to actually accomplish it.

In preparation for our project I viewed dozens of websites from a list of the fastest growing companies in our industry. In each case I started by reviewing the company, its revenue, and a list of their products and services. Then I checked out their website to determine how accurately it reflected their company. When reviewing the websites I used a handful of evaluative questions:

> What is my first impression?
> Does the website adequately describe what the
>   company does?
> Does it make the company feel smaller or larger than their
>   actual revenue size?
> Am I tempted to look further?
> Is the website memorable?
> How does it make me feel about the company?

I was hoping to find a website to inspire our own, but what I discovered surprised me. Most of the websites I reviewed seemed weak and flat compared to the dynamic companies they represented. None—even the huge corporate sites—was particularly memorable. Some, however, did display elements I liked. Sites with a clean look and feel, with easy navigation and clear descriptions of products and services topped my list. So I picked my favorite five websites and presented them to our design company, the Grey Matter Group.

Developing Our New Look

We formed a committee to develop a description of what we were hoping to accomplish with this website of ours. The committee found that we were using our website primarily as a "first impression," attracting a relatively low number of visitors. This was important to understand because the look and feel for this type of site is very different from that of a website used primarily to sell products. Most companies visiting our site were being directed there. They were evaluating us to see if we passed the sniff test. We decided to pursue a site that made a memorable first impression and told visitors what we had to offer.

I told the designers, "We want a prospect viewing our site to lean over to the person in the next cube and say, 'Wow! This is cool! You need to see this site.'" This served as my benchmark for "memorable."

We also wanted the tone of the site to be welcoming, slightly edgy, lighthearted, smart, funny, professional, easy-to-navigate, ultimately enticing the visitor to do business with us. Not a lot to ask, eh? If they could do all of this and make it soar like a bird, we'd be ecstatic!

Having done all this prep work, our next task was to generate an element—a visual—to make the website memorable and provide a lasting impression. We ultimately decided to use the image of a "head" to help people remember us—but no ordinary head would do. The head was meant to convey intelligence, vision, a bit of whimsy, and needed to boast a unique appearance. Otherwise, how would people remember it?

We then set about finding an artist to capture this image. They presented sample drawings from four talented but vastly different artists; we chose artist Eric Feng. Eric's handiwork has since become an iconic image that people associate with our company. We use it on our website, printed marketing materials, online marketing— heck, we even considered it for the cover of this book!

Our graphic features machinelike gears turning inside a human head. Detailed but clean and fluid. We all loved its modern vibe combined with a timeless, universal quality—sort of, Leonardo da Vinci meets Tron. I had underestimated the value of using a professional artist in this process. Working with Eric made the head special, different from anything like it in the world. I would highly recommend using a pro if you're looking to develop a single image to be associated with your company. While a few people have described the head as creepy (sigh), most find it clever, intriguing, and even hip. Regardless, no one can claim it's not memorable!

As you read the above, were you tempted to go to our website? If so—bingo—we've accomplished our objective! A brand-new version of the website has recently replaced the one I describe here. When you look, you will still find the OST head, but more importantly, you will see new innovations and find a cultural commitment to improve and change.

While the OST head provided a smart, edgy visual, our current team embraces the idea that websites are not meant to remain stagnant; they require an individual or team to keep them fresh and relevant. With our most recent website refresh, our marketing and communications team put together a cross-functional group made up of OST employees from various areas of the company and strategic outside partners. They started by interviewing employees, customers, and business partners. Then they used that input to create a look and feel that embraces the foundation of who OST is and also connects with our customers in new ways as more and more people come to our site from online searches.

We have to deliver information about our company, educate our customers, and present our brand in a way that is professional and easy to find. We also need to include other creative updates to establish the new tone and design. We have even launched a new site and brand called OpenDigital, which connects us to an entirely new audience for our services. As I said, a website is like a living creature. It needs to be fed, loved, and cared for if you want visitors to value and engage with it!

Dovetailing our ever-evolving crazy wish list with the need to keep it professional is never an easy task. Our team continues to accomplish this with a conversational, somewhat edgy writing style for all copy on the site. The following paragraph is a good example:

> Every company has a personality. At OST, our positive energy is contagious—open and approachable. We're humble, but confident. Smart, but able to laugh at ourselves when we deserve it. It's true that with more than two decades behind us, we have the experience to help companies do what they do best, even better. And it's true that we're creative collaborators who value innovative thinking and open communication in any project we undertake. When people hear us talk about OST, we want them to simply get that we love our jobs—and the people we work with. Because we do.
>
> —from the OST website, company overview

Readers seem to enjoy our site's fresh, unexpectedly engaging tone. Accessible, but with a little attitude.

What We Blog About

If you do check out our website, you'll notice our company blog focuses on our culture and on our business. People tend to gravitate toward OST because of how we treat our people, and from there they discover how truly good we are at what we do. How we treat our team members reveals a great deal about how we approach relationships with our clients. Our posts are usually written by OST employees, and as with most things at OST, there are no rules. For example, Lizzie Williams from our marketing group wrote the following post:

OST's Magic Recipe for Chicken (Dancing)

192. That's how many tickets I handed out for this year's OST Night at the Ballpark—an annual summer celebration for our Grand Rapids employees and their families. 192! That's 100 more guests than last year!

Growth. That's what we've been experiencing—but not just this year. Every year. As a matter in fact, just last week we found out that OST landed on the Inc. 500 | 5000 list for the seventh year in a row as one of the fastest growing private companies in the US. We recognize this level of exponential growth is unprecedented and are grateful every day for the opportunities it provides, but how does that happen? What's the secret?

Well, I'll say it here, but it's been said hundreds of times before me—we believe that one of the main contributions to our success has been this magical little recipe that our entire organization follows when making all major business decisions:

1. Employees First
2. Clients Second
3. Profits to Follow

Back in 1997 when Hanson was MMMBop-ing on the radio and overalls were überchic, OST was formed. And right from the beginning, the team decided always to make sure that employees' needs were the company's top priority, followed by the clients. They didn't let the neon of the nineties cloud their decision and to this day we are led by a team that understands if you take care of your employees first and your clients immediately following, the profits will fall into place.

So when the seventh-inning stretch rolls around and the chicken dance starts to play, we at OST feel confident that we are part of a family that supports us and respects us as individuals, and we shake our little tail feathers with no hesitation. When you know the company you work for has your back, it's much easier to stand tall and put in your best effort, every day. And that, we believe, is one major reason we have been able to continue to grow and succeed.

Your Website Is Part of Your Corporate Culture

If you want your employees to shake their tail feathers, I encourage you to make sure your website reveals who you really are. Make it something memorable that represents your cultural strengths. If your vision for your website, blog, and social media is different from your cultural reality, you can work on them concurrently. Describe what you envision your ultimate company culture to be with words, then build your culture to match those words with actions.

One word of caution. Don't bend the truth or present a false front that your employees will find out of line with their everyday reality. When writing about the culture, make sure your words accurately portray what your employees see you are striving to accomplish along with what they are experiencing. Your actions need to match what they are reading. Employees are very savvy about how the outside world views their employer. They obviously know what they experience on a daily basis and can tell you if that experience matches up with how the company is representing itself out there.

So leverage your website, blogs, and social media as tools to assist in shaping and promoting your company culture. First impressions last a lifetime and your website is often your prospective client's first impression of you.

Bombarded by Ads

Each day we're bombarded with over three thousand ads in our consumer-saturated society. While few dispute the necessity of marketing, how to market effectively and measure its rate of impact often feels like aiming at a moving target. In the dark. Half the problem is the sheer volume of ads in the marketplace. The other half is in the lack of truth telling. Customers, employees, and leaders alike begin to take marketing spin for granted and view all hype through skeptic-tinted glasses.

Nonetheless I'm still surprised at how many companies overlook the direct impact their website, blogs, and social media campaigns have on their corporate culture—both internally by team members and externally by clients, prospective employees, prospective clients, and the general public.

It can be tough for your marketing voice to stand out amidst the din of the crowd, but this is all the more reason to be as creative, deliberate, and authentic as possible in your strategy and execution. How you communicate who you are and what you do sets the tone for your culture and how you are perceived in the marketplace.

So What Does This Mean to You?

Take a moment now to look at your website—go ahead, it'll only take a few seconds. What is your first impression? Does it represent your company well? Do you think people visiting the site will remember it? Depending on your reaction to these questions, you may need to take action to improve your website. Consider viewing your competitor's sites and the top sites in your industry around the country and around the world. Make a list of the sites that made a favorable impression on you or had an element that might make sense on your site. You can see where your site stacks up to the competition and decide where improving your website fits into your priorities.

Consider creating a visual image, like the OST head, to make your website memorable for visitors and provide a lasting impression. Start by making a list of the cultural characteristics that you would like the image to portray. Use an image that is unexpected; make it stand out amongst the billions of bits that we call the worldwide web.

"NASA Trusts Us, So Can You"

Marketing Techniques That Have Worked Wonders for Us

CHAPTER THEME SONG:
"EYE IN THE SKY,'" THE ALAN PARSONS PROJECT

ORPHEA, a powerful insecticide for spraying outdoors, pulled off one of the most fascinating, gutsy marketing stunts ever. They leased a billboard along a busy highway in Milan, Italy, and went to work. On the left side of the billboard was an ORPHEA spray can aiming to the right with a small caption below that read, "Insecticide for outdoors." Then, starting from the spray nozzle and moving to the right, they applied transparent glue in the shape of a megaphone gradually increasing in width across the entire billboard. As planned, the glue was soon a mass of over one hundred thousand insects in the shape of the imaginary spray coming from the ORPHEA can. It succeeded in attracting millions of views from motorists passing by. No matter what they felt, one thing is for certain, they never forgot it!

When it comes to marketing, don't be afraid to do something interesting and out of the ordinary to capture your target audience's attention. Make your marketing materials, campaigns, and events fascinating so that everyone will remember your company, products, and services. After all, have you ever seen a Super Bowl commercial, the most expensive thirty-second TV spot in the world, that wasn't a little out there?

Conferences, a Questionnaire, and the Long Haul

In the beginning OST focused on the computer systems that run integrated software for large manufacturing companies, what we in the industry call Baan ERP infrastructure. It was an interesting market because manufacturing companies installing Baan were located all over the country. Most start-ups, like OST, do most of their business in the town where they're located. In our first three or four years, however, three quarters of our business was out of state. No one knew much about OST in our early days—a marketing challenge compounded by having our prospective clients spread across multiple states.

Our first attempt at marketing was attending annual Baan conferences and hosting a booth in the vendor area. Initially I was skeptical about these conferences. Like most entrepreneurs, I wanted us to spend all our time and energy "getting the real work done." Thankfully my colleagues perceived the value in these conferences and convinced me to stay the course.

As you might expect, our intense work ethic carried over to these conferences. Year in and year out, we had more prospects spend time in our booth than the thirty or so booths of our competitors. We generally had three or four OST people manning our space and working the crowd. In the weeks leading up to the conference, we strategized how we could get the most out of our investment. We developed an ingenious way to gather prospective contacts and systems information, thereby ensuring our opportunity to start a meaningful conversation. It was a simple card—the size of a business card. On one side it had space for contact information, and on the other side it had a half-dozen questions about their Baan environment.

We would venture into the crowd and say something like, "Would you like to sign up to win an Apple iPod? I just have to ask you a few questions and fill out this card." The answer was almost always yes. In keeping with our company culture, we were pretty positive and full of energy, which made it hard for them to say no. We would proceed to ask their name, the name of their company, and several questions about their Baan implementation. Then we moved in for the kill: "I see you are running Baan on Oracle and Sun? We've done several similar implementations, so let me introduce you to one of our technical folks. I am sure that he can give you some tips that will enhance your implementation." We would hand the prospect off and move on to the next one.

It was incredible how many sales prospects would come from these conversations. We kept a running list and prioritized the leads. The excitement and energy would build throughout the conference and then we would go home exhausted. Back in the office we would assign individuals to follow up on each lead. Every year, we would repeat the same cycle with the same results. Despite making all these great connections, during the first few years of conferences, the actual business we closed was close to zero! What was going on here?

After a while, we started to doubt the value of attending conferences and following up on the associated leads they generated. We were dumbfounded by the number of prospects that would practically award the business to us at the conference and then ignore us when we contacted them afterward. It wasn't until year four or five that we started to reap the benefits of participating in these conferences. We still had the problem of leads not turning into deals, but we were starting to do business with a number of clients we'd met during the first three years. In addition, we were becoming recognized as the leader in Baan infrastructure. Most people at the conference finally knew what we did!

This experience illustrates how marketing works and why often it is hard to measure your ROI in the short term. Everyone says that you need to hear a marketing message seven times before it starts to sink in. That is exactly the kind of thing we experienced with the Baan conferences. By year seven we were clearly recognized as the leader in Baan infrastructure and we have been ever since.

If you are experiencing frustration similar to our Baan conference quandary, be relentless with your strong, consistent message. Eventually people will hear it.

Class Is in Session

As illustrated by our Baan conference example, it's often difficult to determine how much of an impact marketing actually has on sales at any given moment. But for every rule there's an exception. And in this case the exception is when sales are tied directly to marketing. An example would be our Baan classes that we offered for many years.

We launched our first Baan class based on customer demand. It was a two-day seminar that focused on optimizing computer systems for Baan. We charged two thousand US dollars per student to attend. At this price we had to heavily market the benefits to convince students and companies that it would be worthwhile for them to attend. I enjoyed marketing these classes; getting cheeks in seats was a nice diversion from my usual high-pressured work.

We were so successful with this first class that we added four more Baan-related classes and started offering them around the country and later around the world. Since marketing (well, okay, me) was exclusively responsible for filling classes, I learned all kinds of tricks to convince people to attend. We had an online registration system and as soon as someone entered their name in the system I would call them and say, "I saw that you signed into our registration system, so I thought I would call to see if you have any questions." They always seemed pleasantly surprised by the call, and most were thinking about a particular class and almost always had questions. If they were not completely sold on the class by the end of our conversation, I would offer to have them talk with the instructor. My close rate was extremely high.

These classes were profitable for us but also gave us a chance to meet new potential clients and to market OST. Similar to the Baan conferences, we did not get much additional business from companies attending these classes during the first two or three years, but eventually we did. Today we don't offer ongoing education, but I think we should consider it. Education offers all of the benefits already discussed and helps your consultants to stay sharp.

Billboards?

During our first ten years we did little general marketing of our company. We avoided radio, television, news publications, and didn't even have a yellow pages ad (keep in mind, in those days, *every* company had a yellow pages ad). Our reasoning was that we only did business with a few large companies locally so there was no reason to have the general public know about us. And though this may run counter to what you already know about us, we didn't like being in the limelight. This approach worked well until we decided we wanted to go after the midmarket, which included smaller companies.

To jump-start this process, we hired two full-time sales reps to sell into midmarket accounts. It seemed like it would be relatively easy to impress this demographic because we could reference our large household-name clients for credibility. Or maybe not. After the first couple months our reps came to me with a major problem, "No one has ever heard of OST, so it makes it hard to get in the door." Oops. Our policy to keep a low profile had backfired on us. We had to do something to get our name out there quickly.

We tried an aggressive radio campaign and it worked relatively well. We had several people mention that they had heard it. But it wasn't enough—nearly everyone in town still had no idea who we were and what we did. Until one of our midrange reps came to me with an idea—billboards. I liked it and contacted a media guy with whom we'd been working. When I told him about the billboard idea, he said, "Billboards are for companies that want to sell something at the next exit like a hamburger or a cup of coffee, products usually sold to the masses. You will not sell anything by putting a billboard up." I explained that we were not expecting to sell anything, that we just wanted people to recognize our name. He still didn't buy it, but it made all the sense in the world to me.

OST's First Billboard

Our seven-billboard campaign featured the OST head with the headline, "NASA Trusts Us for I.T." with smaller print below, "Local Presence. Global Expertise." A few people were concerned that we might be asked to take the billboards down because we did not have NASA's permission to use their name. I wasn't worried. First of all, who could we ask at NASA for permission? And second, if NASA asked OST to take the billboards down, it would certainly make the news. We would likely get more name recognition from the news than we would from the billboards!

The response from our billboards was beyond anything we could have dreamed; it seemed like everyone saw our signs. To this day, I still believe that the NASA billboards are what put OST on the map. If you are confident in a marketing campaign and you get pushback—trust your instincts just like NASA trusts OST—and go for it.

A Presentation That Focuses on Why

Another obvious but effective way we've marketed OST successfully comes from having a tight, laser-focused presentation. I've probably delivered it over a hundred times—no exaggeration—and it seems to work every time. It's about eight PowerPoint slides long with an overview of the company, OST focus areas, the OST difference, a list of skill sets, a list of household name clients, and a list of awards. The response to this presentation has been outrageously positive.

I start by taking people through the basic history of OST, the number of years in business, physical locations, growth statistics, and financial information—the same thing that every company does. Then I describe the services we provide—up to this point the presentation is about what you would expect.

Then it gets interesting. I say something like, "Every company likes to think that they are different, but our clients tell us we are different. We have brilliant technologists who thrive on complex architecture and challenges; we call them one percenters. If we crammed one hundred systems architects in this room, along with Jim Razmus, Jim would be the best in the room. And we have one percenters in every area of our business. When we decide to add a networking engineer, we find the absolute best networking engineer in the marketplace, then we recruit and hire her. We have done this many times. You might think based on the one percenter description that we are arrogant, but we are just the opposite. That is what's different about OST; our people are genuine and want to please our clients. It is this combination of brilliant and genuine that makes us different."

Next, I talk about our culture of prioritizing our people and their families, the things we do to make OST a fun place to work, and our employee satisfaction levels. It's at this point that someone usually says, "Do you have any openings?" I love it when they say this because it shows that they have bought into our culture.

Then I go on to cover our skill sets, share some household names that we have done business with, and in the early years I would show a list of awards. I always downplayed the awards in the presentation, but I felt that we needed them for credibility. Over the past couple years, we have eliminated that last bit and replaced it with our company video.

If I do it right—poignant pauses, using my hands, meaningful voice inflections, and all the other master presenter tricks of the trade—the audience feels a shiver or two. By the end of the presentation, they are warmed up and can't wait to start doing business with us. Well, not exactly. But in all seriousness, it does accomplish our objective of having them understand and like what OST is all about. And in most cases they do choose to do business with us.

The odd thing is that my business partner, Jim, and I always suspected that the presentation was lacking. It didn't feel like it adequately conveyed the services we provide and the benefits that we brought to our clients. On the one hand, the presentation was always successful and produced the results that we were looking for. On the other hand, it didn't provide the conventional information that we thought our clients should be looking for—and it felt the weaker for it. It wasn't until I read the book *Start with Why* by Simon Sinek that I realized our clients were buying into our "why" and wanted to do business with us because they believe in what we are all about. The presentation was actually spot-on.

This refreshing revelation taught us an important lesson. If your marketing is working—it's okay not to change it just for the sake of perceived improvement. After all, it's hard enough to fix the stuff that isn't working!

Keep Asking the Right Questions

Most fishermen will agree that a smallmouth bass fights pound for pound as much or more than any fish you can catch. I believe that our current marketing staff of three people produces as much or more than any department at OST or any other company. A few years back we tracked our three-person marketing staff's accomplishments for the year: twenty-six articles in seven different publications, nine radio interviews, one TV spot, nine billboards in three cities, twenty-one OST events, nine special projects, seventy-two newsletters, six awards, and much more. This incredible amount of output is all about the passion they have for the company and what they do.

Obviously, I am tremendously proud of our marketing team, but we could double the amount of our output and still miss the mark. The secret to our success is continually challenging ourselves and asking questions like, "Is our message consistent with our culture?" and "Are we having a positive impact on sales?" and "Is everything we do of the highest quality possible?" Marketing's job is to serve the entire organization and deliver results—everything that the public sees is a direct reflection on our company. In business, perception is reality and we help cultivate public perception . . . every day.

That's what marketing is all about.

So What Does This Mean to You?

Companies that offer industry education are naturally looked at as industry leaders and experts in their fields. Even a garbage collection company can teach community classes on recycling to differentiate themselves. If you do not currently offer industry education, consider offering your first class taught by one of your employees—especially if you are in an industry where it is unusual to teach classes.

If you want people to know who you are in a community, consider billboards. If your gut tells you that a marketing idea will work, don't look for confirmation from the experts. Give it a shot—even the experts are wrong at times and some of the best ideas are contrary to conventional thinking.

Take a fresh look at your company overview presentation. (And if you don't have one, maybe you need to create one.) Do you think it stands out compared to your competitor's presentations? Do prospects have a desire to do business with you based on the presentation? Consider focusing your presentation more on why you are in business than what it is that you offer; this will truly differentiate you.

PART FIVE

OUR MISTAKES

Learning the Hard Way

Our Achilles' Heel

Why We Have Trouble with Accountability
and What We're Trying to Do about It

CHAPTER THEME SONG:
"THAT'S WHAT FRIENDS ARE FOR," DIONNE WARWICK

After starting a new diet, I altered my drive to work to avoid passing my favorite bakery. I accidentally drove by the bakery this morning, and as I approached a host of goodies greeted me in the front window. This obviously was no accident, so I prayed, "Lord, it's up to you. If you want me to have any of those delicious goodies, create a parking place for me directly in front of the bakery." And sure enough, on the eighth time around the block, there it was!

Holding yourself accountable is difficult enough; holding others accountable takes things to a whole other level. I've dreaded writing this chapter because I knew I'd have to come clean and let you in on our secret—we're not very good at holding people accountable at OST. But since vulnerability and transparency are important parts of our culture, I might as well explore exactly why we struggle with this.

When we were a tribe of fewer than twenty people, it was easy to hold people accountable because we were all communicating with each other every day. None of us had much experience managing people, so we made it a point of hiring team members with drive who didn't require much direction. Of course, we were also a bit green, so when we asked job candidates if they were self-motivated, we actually believed them when they said yes. Now, eighteen years later, after interviewing over a hundred people, I can confidently confirm that zero applicants have answered no to that question. I can also report that a lot of folks are simply not the self-motivated type!

A Problem in Search of a Solution . . . Still

OST is an exciting place to work as we continue to grow and new opportunities abound. One recent opportunity was among the largest in the history of our company. It quickly became a top priority and everyone at OST was well aware of the positive impact that this project could have on all of us. The leadership team gave blank check authority to the account team to do whatever was needed to assure success. The team energetically came back with a plan to provide our client with "insane levels of service"—a new phrase for our company.

The project began, full of promise, and we were on our way. However, a couple months in, the client had minor concerns; they felt we were not communicating effectively with them and some small things were falling through the cracks. This kind of thing is fairly normal for IT projects, but it seemed a little odd given our audacious goal of insane levels of service, but we let it be.

A few months after that, the client came back again with a heightened level of unease. There were commitments not being completed on time. More things were being missed. It just didn't make sense. Our team had committed to, say it together, *insane levels of service*. They were given the resources to make it happen, and yet the customer was reporting a less than acceptable experience.

What went wrong? Was this an accountability, communications, or operational problem? And can we fix it? At least the answer to the last question is consistent at OST. We will always make it right with our clients and jump through flaming hoops to make sure they are happy. This is why our customer satisfaction scores are an astonishing 90+ percent, and our client retention rate is even higher. But it sure would be a lot easier if we could get it right the first time!

No doubt people at OST tried to figure out the problem and initiated procedures to guard against it ever happening again—until the next time it happens. I could go on and on with my theories about using more project management, insuring that one person has ultimate responsibility for the project, improved communication between OST team members or between OST and the client, better planning, enforcing negative consequences for lack of follow-through, and setting reasonable expectations. But my intuition tells me the core problem was and is lack of accountability.

Fixing a problem like this in an "employees and families first" culture is more difficult than in an "autocratic hierarchical" environment for obvious reasons. We have no interest in becoming a dictatorship, so we need to find employee-friendly approaches to problem solving.

If we had asked for client feedback every month in the form of a satisfaction survey, we might have remained on top of any issues before they devolved into complaints. I realize we need to address process issues too, and a regular satisfaction survey might be considered a Band-Aid approach; nevertheless, we have found client satisfaction surveys to be a great way to keep projects on track. This is especially true if enough people have access to the results. They're a simple and effective source of peer accountability—something we have learned from our past experiences. But even to me this solution leaves something to be desired. There must be a better way!

This story ends flat, I know! But I didn't say I have all the answers because I don't. The good news for OST is that we were successful in turning this situation around because a lot of really good people cared. I suppose our people were held accountable in our own soft way, and in the end, we prevailed.

Client Satisfaction Surveys: A Case Study

A few years back one of our favorite long-term clients asked us to bid on a large three-year IT project. We submitted a detailed bid, and soon after I received a call from the company's CIO. She read our high-quality bid response but could tell we hadn't done a similar project of this size before. On the other hand, the other competing bid was from a company that had obviously tackled many large projects. She preferred OST but had concerns about our lack of experience.

I told her OST would "stand behind our work and make it right no matter what" as we have always done, to which she replied, "That isn't good enough." She sighed, "This is a high-visibility project, and I can't afford any bumps in the road. I need your complete assurance that the project will be smooth from beginning to end." I gave my word that the execution would be flawless, and I meant it.

We were awarded the contract. Holy mackerel! Now we had to deliver! So I came up with what I thought was a foolproof way to keep my word. I gathered our group of OST employees responsible for delivering on the project and sat them down in a conference room. I described what the project meant to OST, my commitment to the client, and the survey that the client would respond to every month. I set a goal of 90+ percent client satisfaction—based on the survey results—and rolled out a reward program for achieving our monthly goals.

It worked! Having an external measurement like a monthly client survey that everyone could see kept everyone accountable in a positive way. It took all of the guesswork and finger-pointing out of the equation and kept our people focused on our client's needs. The reward incentives didn't hurt either. The project was one of OST's most successful complex IT projects ever. And most importantly, the client was thrilled.

Mixing the Old with the New

In a people-first business culture like ours, holding everyone accountable can be a challenge. We have a long way to go, but we are employing creative new methods that are in sync with our culture. Using external measurements, like client surveys, is a simple but powerful approach and it works well for us.

We have noticed that our leadership people who were successful at holding people accountable in their previous jobs sometimes struggle to hold people accountable at OST. They buy into the concept of serving their people, but serving them and holding them accountable often leads to an internal struggle. We ask our leadership team to be kind, but when is it okay to be tough? It gets confusing and at times frustrating.

So we're trying a new approach, especially with managers who are struggling to hold others accountable due to implied cultural constraints. We are asking them to think about what made them successful in their previous companies—with regard to employee accountability—and then to consider what components might work in our culture. If it's their management style that has changed, we are asking them to consider going back to the style that worked, but with a twist.

We want them to dip back into that prior management style, but to incorporate the OST way of doing things as well. We are telling them to hold firm to ideals like being thoughtful, like keeping the employees' best interests in mind, helping the employee to grow personally and professionally, and treating the employee with compassion, as if they were a family member. They are not allowed to yell, "You're an idiot and your mother wears combat boots!" Instead we tell them try something a bit more tactful: "I completely understand the difficulty, given your proclivity for monosyllabic words.

By the way, is your mother still into military footwear?" All kidding aside, we will continue to try this new management style approach, and if it doesn't work, we will try something else. We are determined to find ways to hold our people, and each other, responsible.

John Vancil, our director of professional services, once asked, "So how do we hold each other accountable to being accountable?" It's a thought-provoking question, one worth pursuing once we get the basics ironed out. I would like to close by calling out the positives of accountability in a people-first culture.

We have always operated with wide boundaries that allow for creativity and self-realization. We have a small list of nonnegotiables that help people march to the tune of the same tuba player. For example:

- "We will always do the right thing for our clients. Period."
- "People will always be treated with respect."

There is also an enormous amount of trust, admiration, and collaboration at OST, which lends itself to self-accountability.

Occasionally we slip up, but that's okay—we're not perfect. Anybody want a fresh doughnut from the bakery?

So What Does This Mean to You?

Acknowledge the areas that your company struggles with. Address them openly with your leadership team and with your employees. Many companies ignore uncomfortable issues and only talk about the positives. Believe me—your employees know where the company struggles. Your transparency will be refreshing to them and will build trust. But acknowledgement is not enough. Solicit ideas from your employees for addressing issues, take action, and communicate your progress.

Blunders We Don't Like
to Talk About

But I'm Going to Talk about Them Anyway

CHAPTER THEME SONG:
"DIRTY LAUNDRY," DON HENLEY

During the early days of OST, I would personally go on what I called a "burn"—an endurance test that I wouldn't recommend to an enemy let alone a friend. I'd work at a relentless pace, countless hours for months on end, until I hit a brick wall and my body would collapse in a state of total exhaustion and literally shut down. I'd be useless for a week or two while my body recovered, and then I would start the same self-destructive cycle over again. I'm not sure exactly what it was that actually stopped this cycle. It would be nice to point to a moment of enlightenment and share my wisdom, but I think that I was just sick of being exhausted. I still cringe to think about how foolish I was go on these burns and the many mistakes I've made along the way.

However, it feels like most of the lessons from these mistakes could not be learned any other way. And the really tricky part is not becoming overreactive and swinging too far in the opposite direction when something goes wrong. For instance, I believe that business people are generally honest and trustworthy. But it seems as though many business people don't trust each other. Once someone has been burned by a dishonest business transaction, they often become overly cautious, suspecting that others are out to get them. At OST, we choose to trust everyone unless they prove untrustworthy. This philosophy is an important aspect of our culture and has served us well over the years; customers often tell us how much they appreciate the respect and faith we afford them. However, there was one particular time we took this blind trust a little too far . . . and we paid the price.

Pain in the Pocket Book

We were performing professional services for an out-of-state company and the project was going well. However, our client started to get behind on their payments to us. They assured us that they would catch up soon—and of course, we trusted them. The number of billable hours continued to climb. This went on for a couple months and we started to get a little nervous, but we knew that this company was owned by an economically sound corporation. We also had a contract in place that was legally binding so our bases were covered. Our client continued to praise our work—and not pay their bills as months three and four went by.

At this point they owed us $476,000, so we made a decision to put the brakes on the project. Our client was upset and, ironically, used this as another reason not to pay. After reaching out to some corporate friends, we found out that our client was having financial difficulties and also owed money to several other companies. Even in light of this disconcerting news, we refused to panic; we trusted this company's leaders to do the right thing, honor our contract, and pay their bills.

My next plan of action was simply to call their company president, get his commitment to pay, and send our people back out to finish the project. But when I called the president I didn't get a call back. Not only that, but none of our client's people would return our calls. When we did finally make contact, they were defensive and made us out to be the bad guys for pestering them. Now we were afraid, but still felt relatively sure that we would recover the money; they were obviously under an enormous amount of pressure.

Finally, we contacted our attorney and were shocked to find out that we could not go after the parent company if our client defaulted. The company we were contracted with was set up as a separate Limited Liability Corporation (LLC), which would protect the parent company. Our attorney gently informed us, "If the LLC goes bankrupt, you will likely get pennies back on the dollar." Unfortunately, our attorney was spot-on. About six months into the ordeal, we received a certified letter from our client's lawyers offering us eight cents on the dollar. We had little choice; we could take the eight percent or our client would go bankrupt and we would likely get nothing. Our attorney recommended that we take the deal—and we did.

It was a painful experience and a devastating financial loss. Since then we have made changes in our collection policies to prevent this from ever happening again. We are still willing to let companies go thirty days without payment on professional services engagements, but after that we pull our people from the client site until they have paid. We obviously made a big mistake by waiting too long to confront the company, but we refused to let it change our willingness to trust people. Call me old-fashioned (I've been around too long to be called naïve), but I still believe people to be generally honest and trustworthy until they show me otherwise. So our OST culture learned to practice what I like to call "informed trust," a relationship of mutual respect earned by the ongoing display of integrity, honesty, and responsibility.

When Optimism Led Us Astray

We have always been optimistic as a company, and people have been our top priority from the start. But if you combine these two positive ingredients with a dash of inexperience, it can potentially become a recipe for disaster—which is why your culture's positive ingredients must be seasoned with the lessons learned from past mistakes.

We were in one of our overly idealistic mindsets when we hired two fantastic technical people who were great cultural fits. We were a small company at the time and far too optimistic when it came to sales. Our partners would come to us with ideas, and we would ramp up our work force in anticipation of business not yet confirmed.

These new team members quickly became two of our favorite employees with one big catch: we didn't have enough work for them. We knew that we couldn't afford to keep them unless we scared up more work, so I made it my personal mission to do just that. However, I became so focused on finding them work that I lost all perspective on what made sense for the company. Both of these employees had awesome attitudes and were the kind of people that everyone liked to be around. Unfortunately, I was unsuccessful in finding enough for them to do, and ever so gradually we began to see a change in their behavior . . . and the way we felt about them.

After about nine months it became an ugly situation. Imagine having a strong desire to work, with very little to do, and the owners of the small company you work for becoming more and more concerned that you were dragging them down. As you would expect both employees were unhappy and had developed attitude issues. It was upsetting to know that it was completely our fault.

Regretfully, I decided that we had to let them go and dreaded the inevitable discussion. When it finally took place, they were both gracious and understanding. It was almost as if a load was lifted off their shoulders too; it certainly was a load off mine. They were—and still are—great guys. It was OST that messed up. We wanted so badly to protect their jobs that we actually hurt them more than we were helping them. In the years since this happened, we have become much more responsive in making such painful but necessary decisions. It's better for the employees as well as OST and the health of our culture.

Learning from Start-Up Flops

OST's first attempts at geographic expansion were a disaster. We have always prided ourselves in our level of business diversification at OST. Prior to doing so geographically, we had diversified by industry verticals (Healthcare, Finance, and Manufacturing), product mix (Hardware, Software, and Services), and product life-cycle stages (Introduction, Growth, and Maturity.) We felt that diversification was our best proactive defense against layoffs. Since our culture is all about our people and their families, we did everything possible to prevent job loss. This level of diversification positioned us for stability and helped us weather the storm when the great recession hit.

Ten years ago, we were pleased with our level of diversification, except when viewed from a geographic perspective. We were solely located in the state of Michigan; one of the most economically depressed states in the nation at the time, and wanted to expand into at least one other state to reduce our overall risk.

At that time OST was a member of a national index group of information technology service providers that met quarterly to share strategies and ideas. Having been cautioned about the various challenges of geographical expansion by industry experts, we approached our index group to get members' opinions.

They confirmed that expanding into another state was extremely difficult, but several of them had successfully done it. Based on their experience, they recommended that we acquire a small business in the new location or have a senior level person from OST move to the new location . . . or both. One company's success was the result of hiring a seasoned executive who had already opened offices for other companies; alas, this option was too expensive for us. Another company owned an airplane, which allowed them to travel to their new office in an adjoining state a few times per week; this was also not an option. No money. No pilot. We listened to all these recommendations but in the end decided to do it our own way.

We opted to hire entrepreneurial-minded sales people in several Midwest cities with the hope that, if we planted enough seeds, at least one might take root. Then we could concentrate on developing that little sprout into a successful, thriving office. So we hired sales people in Detroit, Cleveland, Cincinnati, Indianapolis, Atlanta, Chicago, and Minneapolis. We sat back and waited for one of these locations to take off. Ahem. None of them did.

After about five years of false starts and as much futility, we decided to take the original advice of the index group and send one of our senior level people to a new location to manage it. We also made a long-term commitment that included frequent leadership visits to provide encouragement and lend hands-on support. Happily, this intense focus on one location worked. Within four years, OST Minneapolis was profitable and contributing mightily to our bottom line. Since then we have opened OST Chicago and OST Detroit and are building momentum in both of these locations as well.

We like to do things our own way, but there are certainly times when it makes sense to learn from others.

We have also questioned our original motives for expanding back then. Adding a new office to diversify geographically was fine because it was part of our strategy to protect our people from layoffs, but we were missing something. Today, when we consider moving into new geographies, it's our intention that extending our reach might allow those locations to enjoy OST's unique business culture in their own work environments. We believe that looking at growth through this new lens, and combining this mindset with the proven approaches discussed earlier, increases our odds of future success.

Talk about Your Mistakes

As a business leader, you naturally want your company and its culture to grow and thrive. It comes as no surprise that the path to growth, maturity, and health includes a few detours, potholes, and dead ends. The challenge is adjusting course and learning from these mistakes and miscalculations. We don't like to talk about our mistakes, especially the ones that shine with the megawatt glare of "what were we thinking?" in hindsight. But examining mistakes out in the light of day will provide illumination when the road turns dark the next time.

So What Does This Mean to You?

Business people are generally trustworthy, so don't let one or two difficult situations let you become cynical. Trust everyone that feels trustworthy, but use common sense and good business practices when it comes to money collection—"informed trust."

When making difficult decisions such as letting people go, don't procrastinate, dragging out situations like this has the potential for more harm than good for both the employer and the employee.

One of the best things you can do for the health of your business is diversification, regardless of your business culture. Diversifying your business in areas like products, services, industries, and geographies provides stability and helps you to weather the storm of economic downturns.

There is a time to do things your own way and learn from your mistakes. Geographical expansion is not one of them. When making big decisions, learn from other companies that have made similar decisions in the past. No reason to reinvent the wheel.

·· (23) ··

Conclusion

Is It Time to Change Your Culture?

CHAPTER THEME SONG:
"A CHANGE WOULD DO YOU GOOD," SHERYL CROW

One day a florist went to a barber for a haircut. After the cut, he asked about his bill, and the barber replied, "I cannot accept money from you. I'm doing community service this week." The florist was pleased and left the shop. When the barber went to open his shop the next morning, there was a thank-you card and a dozen roses waiting for him at his door.

Later, a police officer comes in for a haircut, and when he tries to pay his bill, the barber again replies, "I cannot accept money from you. I'm doing community service this week." The policeman was happy and left the shop. The next morning when the barber went to open up, there was a thank-you card and a dozen donuts waiting for him at his door.

Then his Congressman came in for a haircut, and when he went to pay his bill, the barber again replied, "I cannot accept money from you. I'm doing community service this week." The Congressman was very happy and left the shop. The next morning, when the barber went to open up, there were a dozen Congressmen lined up waiting for free haircuts.

Contrary to popular thought, there is no such thing as a "free lunch." If you really want transformational business culture change, you'll need to give it everything you've got; it has to come from your heart and your soul.

And you need to put others before yourself at work and in your community. The story below symbolizes the type of business culture that I have done my best to describe throughout this book.

Lake Michigan for the First Time

We encourage employees to look for organic opportunities that come their way. We challenge them to think just as creatively about these efforts as they do about problem solving at work.

Maybe there's no better example of creative community service than this crazy idea we had a couple years ago. We wanted to give inner-city kids the opportunity to see Lake Michigan. Our corporate office is located only forty-five minutes from the "Big Lake," as it's called. If you're not familiar with its beauty and grandeur, it feels more like the ocean than most lakes you see. Lined with sand dunes it boasts some of the most spectacular beaches in the world. Believe it or not, Lake Michigan is so big that people actually surf on it. I grew up in Michigan and have been privileged to travel out to the lakeshore almost every summer since I was a kid.

Imagine our surprise when I learned *90 percent* of children in the very neighborhood where our office is located had never been to Lake Michigan. We couldn't believe it—to be so close to something so vast and beautiful and never have seen it. We vowed I would find a way to get these kids to Lake Michigan!

We talked about our idea with coworkers, family, business acquaintances, pastors, and anyone that would listen. More than a few people argued that bringing a bunch of kids out to Lake Michigan wouldn't accomplish anything. Some suggested that we bring them to a local university instead, so they might connect with the idea of attending college someday. While we appreciated the feedback, we still believed that there was value in having these kids see Lake Michigan. We wanted to expose them to something remarkable that was within reach. A place they could visit again, if they wanted. A place that would spark their imagination and fuel their dreams—revealing how much more of life awaited them beyond the few city blocks where they currently lived.

At first, we would just solicit volunteers from our company, line up some cars, load the kids in, and bring them to the Lake. How hard could it be? Okay, we were somewhat naïve. Taking a bunch of children out of grade school requires permission from their parents, an educational component, and several levels of approval. Luckily, John Helmholdt, a school official, loved the idea—and the kids—so was willing to go to bat for us.

It took almost a year to organize, but the following spring, OST sponsored four busloads of fifth graders—over two hundred kids—from our west-side neighborhood to see Lake Michigan. Mike Lomonaco, OST marketing manager, rode on one of the buses and asked how many kids had seen Lake Michigan. Among fifty-one young passengers, only two raised their hands. The numbers were similar on other buses.

Once they arrived, it was time for the big reveal. The school district had arranged for park rangers from Hoffmaster State Park to host the kids and provide education on the lake and surrounding natural habitat. One of the rangers had the children stand on the inland side of the sand dune before leading them to a majestic view of Lake Michigan. He asked each of them to remain still and just listen. After the silence, one of the little girls said, "I have never heard it so quiet before." Her west-side city neighborhood was constant activity and noise. Next, the park ranger asked the kids to hike to the top of the dune to see the Big Lake. Expecting the kids to yell and run down, splashing in the water, we were stunned as they stood at the top—mouths closed and eyes wide.

Today, we insure that every fifth-grader in Grand Rapids Public Schools gets a trip to Lake Michigan. That is about 1,200 kids each year!

There are so many needs in our communities and so few hours. Rallying our companies around a cause is a sure way to encourage camaraderie among our employees and enrich our company cultures. Next year we plan to double the number of students we'll take to Lake Michigan, but my dream is so much bigger than that.

There are countless inner-city neighborhoods in the world where children have never seen their "Lake Michigan." Kids in Arizona who have never seen the Grand Canyon, kids in LA who have never seen the Pacific Ocean, kids in Boston who have never seen the harbor, and the list goes on and on. Wouldn't it be incredible if even a fraction of those kids could see "it," to give them a glimpse of hope for something better? Like those students atop the dune seeing Lake Michigan for the first time, the possibilities leave us in awe.

This Lake Michigan experience and many like it are clearly outcomes of the OST business culture. Build your own "Kitchen" and many will come to the table and many will be satisfied.

So What Does This Mean to You?

Is your business culture a top priority? If so, pick one or two ideas from this book and start implementing them today.

Epilogue

My Story

CHAPTER THEME SONG:
"IT'S MY LIFE," BON JOVI

I was born in a quaint Midwestern town, the son of an alcoholic house painter (I know what you're thinking; no, he did not drink before climbing ladders.) And why does this matter?

You've gotten to know a little about who I am and how I came to cofound and lead OST. But in order to understand why people matter so much in our company's culture, I think you need to know some of my personal story. So indulge me, as I tell you about my life so that you can see for yourself that even a blind squirrel can eventually find a nut if he keeps looking and learning along the way.

My dad was a good man with a great heart, but in the end his drinking got the best of him. He was the youngest of nine children, raised in a country setting, and the son of a second-generation German immigrant. He endured an abusive childhood, although he rarely said much about it. Somehow, he made it through tenth grade, but probably shouldn't have. It wasn't until I was an adult and saw my dad trying to sound out the simplest words in a baby book, while reading to his granddaughter, that I realized he didn't know how to read. He had kept this secret from us all

*One of My Childhood Homes
in Grand Haven, Michigan*

of our lives. He must have suffered the shame of this his whole life—looking back now, it helps me to better understand him.

My father loved me deeply, but he never really liked me much. Overall my childhood memories are pleasant, with a few rough spots, but let's just say my home environment and life experiences didn't foster a lot of self-confidence. Dad provided well for us from a financial perspective—he was good at business as we come from a long line of entrepreneurial types. My mom was loving, supportive, and did the best she possibly could, but my dad dominated the mood in the house—good or bad, but due to his alcoholism, mostly bad. My mom, who married my dad on her seventeenth birthday, provided me with love, nurturing, support, and a sense of adventure. My mom and dad were both hard workers, and they taught me to be trustworthy, honest, fair, and diligent like they were. Their greatest gift was developing in me an intense drive to succeed.

The Joy of . . . Shoveling Sand?

Every summer for one week I would go with my mom, aunt, cousins, grandmother, and great-grandmother to a different cottage on a lake in northern Michigan. I have fond memories of swimming all day and playing board games at night. These were some of the best times of my life.

I attended prayer meetings with my mom at my grandmother's house when I was ten years old. Every Tuesday, twenty or thirty women would gather together and pray (with little Danny listening intently)—these ladies were some of the most amazing, caring people I have ever met. I accepted Christ as my Lord and Savior during this time in my life, which has shaped my life more than any other experience. I do not advertise my faith in my daily work life, but it would not be right to tell my life story and leave out this fact.

Starting at age fifteen, I worked for dad during my summers off school. He always gave me the crappy jobs like scraping, sanding, and shoveling sand, but he instilled in me a powerful work ethic that has stuck to this day. I learned to shovel sand for an entire day and find satisfaction in my accomplishment. I truly believe that this is the biggest secret to my entrepreneurial success. You have to find a way to care about what you're doing no matter how trivial it may seem at the time. Even if the job is small, the habits you develop from taking pride in your work have enormous impact.

Gaining Confidence

Working on the job for my dad was actually fun at times—especially when he was in a positive mood. Working at home was a different story. My dad would regularly have me clean the garage on Saturday mornings, and no matter how hard I worked, it was never good enough. Years later I would find myself still trying to prove to him that the garage couldn't be any cleaner.

When I turned sixteen, I was privileged to work with a good man named Gordy Wyant during those long, hot summer days painting for my dad. Mr. Wyant was my drafting teacher in ninth grade and much beloved by everyone as a patient teacher and a positive man of faith. The opportunity to work side by side with him during the summers of my high school years was a big deal to me.

After high school I worked full-time for two years as a real estate appraiser for the city of Grand Haven, Michigan. I had the privilege of working for a young city assessor named John Petoskey. John and his wife, Sally, both in their early thirties and grads of Michigan State University, had a zest for life. They took me under their wing and introduced me to a new world, things I would never have experienced otherwise. I was invited to go sailing frequently, they involved me in their family gatherings, and were the first to treat me to a night out at a fancy restaurant. I remember Sally teaching me to spread the napkin on my lap and explaining why there were so many forks and spoons.

John was a really smart guy and fun to be around, but our jobs were stressful because we regularly had to deal with people who were upset about their increase in assessments. In February we gave people an opportunity to appeal their assessments and designated five days for taxpayers to meet with us informally to discuss their issues a couple weeks before the board of review. If they were still unhappy, they could take their problem a step further and meet with the official board of review panel.

I participated in both the informal meetings and the board of review. On the days we held the informal meetings John was in one office and I was in another, and we met individually with one disgruntled person after another all day long. People were waiting in the hallway every day until five o'clock when we closed the doors and headed home exhausted. You'd think I would have dreaded meeting with all those ornery folks, but I actually liked the challenge.

I took pride in the quality of my appraisal work. I felt our approach to appraising was professional and well-reasoned. When people met with us, they were pretty steamed, often coming in with both barrels blazing—only figuratively, I'm happy to say. To me, it was all a big game. My objective was to educate them on our thoughtful methodology and have them feel that they were treated fairly. In some cases, their arguments were valid, and I was quick to change the assessed value accordingly. Regardless, I found that I was very good at keeping my cool and making people feel a whole lot better about their assessment. I fulfilled a similar role during the board of review. These experiences gave me some much needed confidence to handle conflicts and find appropriate resolutions, which would serve me well later in my career.

New Beginnings

John and Sally believed in me even when they saw me making occasional bad choices, like staying out too late and having a little too much "fun." John believed in me as a person, but he also believed in me professionally, so before long he and Sally began encouraging me to attend a four-year college. I was already taking classes in the evening at a local community college, but had not accumulated many credits and didn't have a long-term plan. Passionate alumnae, John and Sally thought I should apply to Michigan State. I wrote this idea off as crazy, never daring to consider something this big, let alone act on it.

During this period in my life I also became the treasurer of our small country church. I was deathly afraid of speaking in front of people, but the pastor asked me a couple weeks in advance to present the treasurer's report to the congregation.

When that Sunday arrived, I was an emotional wreck. While less than forty people attended, I froze when I got up to give the report. My heart felt like it would beat right out of my chest and my legs and hands were shaking uncontrollably. I tried to speak, but nothing came out. Shamefully, I walked back to my pew and sat down; I never did give that treasure's report to the church. After this devastating experience, my inability to speak publicly became an obsession.

After a couple years of working full-time for the city and much encouragement from John and Sally, I decided to apply to Michigan State. By June I received a notice from the university stating that I was wait-listed until they could review my latest semester of community college grades. My high school grades alone were mediocre, not nearly good enough for me to be accepted into MSU. It was summertime, and if accepted, I would be starting that fall.

In a strange sort of way, I was relieved not to get a definitive answer because I was so afraid of the changes that would come if I entered MSU. I would be a couple years older than the other students, and I didn't have a roommate lined up, which meant I would be assigned one at random.

There was another reason for my ambivalence about attending college full-time. While I had been dating girls regularly since graduating from high school, none of them had held my interest for long . . . until lately. Barb was a bank teller I saw on a weekly basis when I deposited the offerings from church, as one of my duties as church treasurer. We had chatted casually for a while, and I finally asked her out. We started dating at the beginning of July and just two weeks later, I knew she was the one.

In August a second letter arrived in the mail with an MSU return address, and I knew it would contain the university's decision. If they rejected me, I did not have an alternative plan, except to stay in Grand Haven as my parents and their parents had done. If the university accepted me, I would have to leave Barb and head into a scary new world that I knew nothing about.

I opened the letter from Michigan State and held my breath. I couldn't believe it. "Congratulations on becoming an MSU Spartan." I literally jumped for joy! I had made the cut, but only by the narrowest of margins. After the initial excitement of my acceptance, I click-clacked up the hill of my emotional roller coaster—still excited, but also afraid of the unknown and sad to be leaving Barb.

When I announced my intention to attend Michigan State University, my father asked, "Why would you want to do that when you already have a good job?" Apparently the idea of attending college was threatening to him. My mom encouraged me as she always had but didn't really understand anything about college.

Then I learned that Mr. Wyant, my old painting buddy and school teacher, had told one of my best friends that I didn't have what it takes to succeed at Michigan State. I was devastated, but chose to use this knowledge as positive incentive to prove Mr. Wyant wrong.

That fall I left for East Lansing without a roommate assignment, which only served to increase my anxiety. However, I soon learned that I had more significant worries, realizing I was ill-prepared for the academic demands that lay ahead. I was in way over my head. As the time passed, I developed some wonderful lifelong friendships, somehow managed to put myself through school financially, and emerged after four years with a degree and a wife. (Barb and I were married the summer before my senior year—over thirty years ago!)

I was on my way to a new life, one beyond the town where I'd grown up.

The Most Difficult Year of My Life

After graduating from MSU, with honors (remember, I learned to work hard when shoveling sand), I left for Poughkeepsie, New York—two hours north of New York City—to work for IBM. I worked for a former football player named Nigel Davis whose hand was so large that it swallowed up my own oversized paw. Nigel was one of the most inspirational people I had ever met or ever will meet. He told us we were his Green Berets of subcontract procurement—the best of the best—and we believed it.

Despite all the support, that first year with IBM turned out to be the most difficult of my life. I was suffering from major anxiety. After all, I had gotten married, moved from Michigan to New York, had a child on the way, was battling stomach health issues, and started an intensely demanding job with IBM—all within the same year. To top it all off, my dad's alcoholism was taking its toll on my parents' marriage, which affected us as well. I met with a psychologist who told me that the combination of these life events would make just about anyone lose it. This made me feel a little better (I think), but my emotional struggles were still debilitating. I continued to meet with this psychologist, weekly for the next year, and took medications, like Valium, just to get through each day.

We spent a total of three and a half years in New York State, and despite my anxiety levels, I was promoted multiple times. I also decided to face my fear of public speaking head on by taking a course and searching out opportunities to speak at work. I was still a nervous wreck in front of people, but I was sick of living in fear. I had to face my fears if I truly wanted to move forward.

Sales School Hell

During that time in New York, my wife, Barb, and I had two children. Heidi was age three, and Kyle was one when we were offered the chance to move back to Michigan with IBM. The idea of returning was appealing because we could be near family for the kids. The only drawback was that I would be required to change careers within IBM to become a computer systems engineer. We decided to go for it.

Our first year back in Michigan was another challenging one for me. I attended IBM's world famous sales training facilities in Atlanta, Georgia, and later in Dallas, Texas. It was a full year of intense training that went something like this: take self-study courses for six weeks, go to class in Atlanta for two weeks, take self-study courses for eight weeks, go to class in Atlanta for three weeks, take self-study courses for eight weeks, go back to Atlanta for another three weeks, then study for four weeks and go to a Dallas class for two weeks.

The Atlanta-based sales classes were brutal. Upon arrival, each student took an exam that covered the material they had been studying over the past weeks. If you passed the test, you stayed; if you failed, they escorted you back to your room and then to the airport to fly back to your branch office. They added the airport escort when someone committed suicide by hanging themselves in their room from the shame of failing the exam.

Needless to say, I didn't handle this type of pressure well and was not one of the more promising students. While I thought I had done quite well on my first mock sales call, apparently, I had missed more than two points on IBM's intricately measured rating system and therefore failed the test. My mentor informed me that he would be calling my manager in Michigan "just to let her know that I hadn't passed." He also let me know that the other students would be feeling sorry for me in the group meeting that afternoon.

It seemed like an eternity waiting for the group meeting. When the time finally came, my mentor shared my news of failure with the team. He played a video of the call in front of us and ridiculed my performance; it hurt deeply when he laughed in a condescending way at my mistakes. Then he stated that he and I were going to recreate the call for them right then and there. I was terrified, fumbling my words repeatedly—I never did get it right as he drilled me over and over again. I felt like a wounded animal as he finally relented; his prediction was right, I could see the pity in all of their eyes.

Grief and Pain

It would be easy to write an entire book based on tales from that one year of sales school, but it would serve no purpose. The point is that I made it through that year and my experiences served to further shape me—for better or for worse. One thing was certain, if I could make it through this, I could make it through anything. I was less afraid of everything after attending this school.

Every day at IBM, we dressed in either a blue or gray suit, white button down shirt, and black wing tips; we spiced it up a little with our ties—surprisingly, stripes, prints, and most colors were allowed. My first role in Michigan was as a systems engineer supporting Tom McDonald, one of our most aggressive sales people. I learned a lot from Tom—he was smart and fearless with energy to burn. But two years later, when I was promoted to a sales position, I learned that Tom had told others that he didn't believe I'd succeed in this new position. What was it with these guys? I had proven Mr. Wyant wrong about Michigan State; now I was more determined than ever to do the same here.

I did, in fact, flourish in my new role as a sales person at IBM, but I always felt like a round peg in a square hole—like I was trying to be somebody that I wasn't. This helped me realize that what I really wanted was to start my own business. Since I didn't have the wherewithal to do it at that time, I decided to leverage my ten years of experience with IBM and take a full commission sales position for a computer leasing company called G/S Leasing. By this time, our third child, Jill, had been born, three years after Kyle. Barb was a stay-at-home mom, so any additional income I earned would be welcome.

Sometime during my five-year stint with G/S, my dad died of cirrhosis of the liver at the age of fifty-nine. I will never forget the courage of the female doctor who brought my two brothers and me together at the time of my father's death. "I want you boys to know that your dad died from alcoholism. People will try to cover it up, but the reality is that I could not stop the bleeding because his liver was no longer functioning. I thought each of you deserved to know the truth so that you can make your own decisions about drinking." I wish I knew who this doctor was so that I could thank her today.

About a month later I received a certified letter in the mail from my dad's attorney, and it read something like: "I am of sound mind and acknowledge that I have three children Dan, Kevin, and Todd. My entire estate is to go to Kevin and Todd, and Dan is to get nothing."

We all face difficult things in life, and this was one of mine. It wasn't losing the money that hurt; it was the fact that I was effectively being disowned by my own father. I didn't cry, but I probably should have. I believe that my dad had a great heart and deep down was a good person, but the alcohol had gotten the better of him.

I channeled my grief into work and learned a lot about building a business while working for G/S Leasing. Nothing was going to stop me from being successful. I made cold call after cold call as I ramped up my business. I was way out of my comfort zone, and there were some shaky voice cracking calls that I hoped nobody would remember. But I kept at it!

On the Way to a Dream

At the same time I was ramping up my business at G/S, I tried my hand at entrepreneurial start-ups on the side. The first was SkyTech International, a company that offered Internet via satellite services. Unfortunately, we were way too early in the business cycle, as people had no idea what the Internet was yet. It failed miserably. The business lost about $30,000, a fortune to me at the time. My second attempt was Affordable Systems, a used-computer business. I purchased personal computers coming off lease, cleaned them up, reloaded the operating system, and sold them to businesses. Affordable Systems was mildly profitable, but not something I wanted to do for the long haul. Both of these businesses were great learning experiences that would serve me well later.

While I was struggling at times with SkyTech International and Affordable Systems, my sales business at G/S Leasing was taking off. Much of this success I owed to a great businessman named Steve Nagengast, an executive at a company with whom we partnered. Steve was sharp, well liked, and did business with integrity. He encouraged me and helped me build relationships with his sales reps so that I could support their business and leverage the sales of my computer leases.

The owners of G/S Leasing knew I was involved in side businesses, but since I was their top new account rep for five years in a row, they didn't say much about it. Eventually, Mike Maiman, the chairman of G/S Leasing, and Steve Nagengast got together and decided to have G/S open a new computer hardware business to support one of Steve's new ventures.

They asked me to launch the business, which I was thrilled to do. However, a year later I heard through the grapevine that Steve thought I was a great sales rep, but didn't think I had what it took to run a business. By this point in my career, I was used to being underestimated. I highly respected Steve and thought the world of him, so I used this comment—along with others from the past—as gasoline on the fire of determination burning inside me.

The next time I looked up, I was living out my dream through the birth of OST, which I described in detail earlier. The first six or seven years were tough like every entrepreneurial start-up. The last eleven years have been by far the best working years of my life. I literally looked forward to going into work every day. I credit the love of work to all the incredible people that I work with and our insatiable desire to build the best business culture. Almost two decades have flown by, and I've handed off the baton to new leaders at OST.

But my story is far from over. I've already started several new ventures and can't wait to see where they take me. I'm living proof that you can do anything you set your mind to do, no matter who says otherwise. If you work hard, put your relationships with positive people first, and are tenacious in your efforts, then your success is guaranteed. Tell 'em Dan said so.

Made in the USA
Middletown, DE
02 December 2021